Twayne's United States Authors Series

EDITOR OF THIS VOLUME

Kenneth Eble
University of Utah

Constance M. Rourke

TUSAS 412

Constance M. Rourke

CONSTANCE M. ROURKE

By SAMUEL I. BELLMAN
California State Polytechnic University, Pomona

TWAYNE PUBLISHERS

A DIVISION OF G.K. HALL & CO. BOSTON

Copyright © 1981 by G.K. Hall & Co.

Published in 1981 by Twayne Publishers
A Division of G.K. Hall & Co.
All Rights Reserved

Printed on permanent/durable acid-free paper and bound
in the United States of America

First Printing

Library of Congress Cataloging in Publication Data

Bellman, Samuel Irving, 1926-
Constance M. Rourke.

(Twayne's United States authors series ; TUSAS 412)
Bibliography p. 155–58
Includes index.
1.   Rourke, Constance Mayfield, 1885–1941. 2. Americanists—
United States—Biography.
E175.5.R8B44   973'.072024 [B]   80-29145
ISBN 0-8057-7341-X

For Jeanne, Joel Ethan, and Jonathan David

Contents

About the Author

Samuel I. Bellman was born and raised in El Paso, Texas, received his B.A. from the University of Texas (Austin) in 1947, his M.A. from Wayne University (Detroit) in 1951, and his Ph.D. from The Ohio State University (Columbus) in 1955. A Professor of English at California State Polytechnic University, Pomona, he has taught at various other academic institutions in the United States and spent the academic year 1975–1976 in England, as Visiting Exchange Professor at Portsmouth Polytechnic in Portsmouth, Hampshire.

His publications include a Twayne U.S. Authors biography of Marjorie Kinnan Rawlings; numerous essays and reviews dealing with modern American literature (many of these have been reprinted wholly or in part, in the Gale Research Company's *Contemporary Literary Criticism* series); encyclopedia and literary-sourcebook articles on Rawlings, Rourke, and other American writers; several dozen poems which have appeared in journals and poetry collections; and two collections of essays which he edited for Freshman Composition courses: *The College Experience* and *Survey and Forecast.*

Preface

It is challenging to prepare a study of Constance Mayfield Rourke at this time. Although she dedicated her life to an examination of American culture and folk art, laboring diligently for over thirty years until her death in 1941, she has received less attention than she deserves. A fairly recent Yale doctoral dissertation in history, Joan S. Rubin's *A World Out of a Wilderness: Constance Rourke and the Search for a Usable Past* (1974), adapted for publication in 1980 under the title *Constance Rourke and American Culture,* indicates, however, that there is still scholarly interest in her writings. Rubin's work, which deals with Miss Rourke's unpublished papers as well as her published writings, considers among other things the author's attempts to show that contrary to the earlier complaints of Van Wyck Brooks, our country really did have a rich store of cultural materials and traditions for writers to draw upon. I shall not rehash here the complicated yet amiable dispute over America's nurture of her creative individuals, and Rourke's critical views relative to those of such critics as Brooks, Parrington, DeVoto, Mumford, Matthiessen, etc.; Rubin covers these matters at length. Rather, I shall provide an extended introduction to Rourke's published works: her two important cultural surveys, *Trumpets of Jubilee* (1927) and *American Humor* (1931); a good biographical sketch of an American artist, *Charles Sheeler;* three other biographical works of far less significance; a volume of posthumously collected essays; and certain of her magazine pieces.

First, however, I wish to place Rourke in a specific cultural and social context. The above writings express her varied interests: (1) native American traditions, (2) the formation of distinct cultural groups, (3) giantism, (4) conserving the old yet "making all things new"—one example of which was post-Calvinist revivalism, and another example was the collecting and recycling of American art forms, and (5) the world of the theater as a special Wonderland.

Where Rourke came from, that is, must precede a consideration of what she accomplished and its significance for American literary studies.

Califorina State Polytechnic University,
Pomona

Acknowledgments

My placing a letter requesting information about Constance Rourke, in the *Grand Rapids Press* early in 1973, brought forth a number of friendly and helpful responses, in the form of periodical clippings, reminiscences, and other materials. I wish to thank Mrs. Benjamin P. Merrick, Ms. Elsie L. Hofmann, Miss Jane O'Connor, and Ms. Dorothy S. Blake for their kind and generous assistance.

Miss L. Louise Des Jardins, whose sister, Mabel Des Jardins (now deceased), happened to have typed all of Rourke's book manuscripts before they were sent to the publisher—Harcourt, Brace and Company—must be accorded very special mention. Not only did this gracious and kind-hearted lady send me numerous clippings and other informational items concerning Rourke, but she gave me three presentation copies (autographed first editions with personal expressions of gratitude) of Rourke books which the author had long ago given to Miss Mabel Des Jardins: *Troupers of the Gold Coast, Davy Crockett,* and *Charles Sheeler*—the last bearing not only Rourke's autograph and presentation note, but Charles Sheeler's autograph as well.

Fortunately, I was able to spend a day in Grand Rapids, on April 12, 1973, as the guest of Miss Des Jardins and her friend, Miss Cecilia Link, who met me at the airport and very kindly drove me all over town so that I could get the feel of Rourke's home base. Thus I was able to see the home where Rourke and her mother had lived for so many years, a two-and-a-half-story clapboard house located at 111 Luton Avenue, S.E. We also visited Woodlawn Cemetery, where both mother and daughter are buried, and saw Constance Rourke's gravestone and the headstone for her mother and herself. In addition, we went to the offices of the *Grand Rapids Press* so that I could look over the newspaper files for material on Rourke; here I wish to thank the editorial department of the *Press* for allowing me to do so. Finally, we explored various locales in Grand Rapids, particularly the

Grand Rapids Public Museum, the Gaslight Village of which (with its collection of furniture, costumes, and other relics of bygone days) would I am certain have meant much to Rourke. I am grateful for additional kindnesses from these good ladies. Miss Link later sent me a number of color prints of the Rourke home and the grave markers of the Rourke ladies. Miss Des Jardins wrote me many interesting letters about her life in Grand Rapids.

Mrs. William J. (Linda) Butler of Tucson, Arizona also merits very special mention. A longtime intimate friend of Constance Rourke in Grand Rapids, and an artist sharing many of Rourke's interests in art projects and exhibits there, Mrs. Butler was named administratrix of her estate after Rourke died on March 23, 1941. She wrote me many letters about Rourke, and when I visited her in Tucson, in June of 1973, she very generously made available to me her collection of Rourkeiana. Mrs. Butler provided me with a wealth of background material, graciously entertained my family, and enlivened my research with fascinating reminiscences of the two Rourke ladies. Mrs. Butler also gave me two informative biographical sketches, one written by Mrs. Margaret Marshall, a New York City journalist who was also a very close friend of Rourke, and the other written by Miss Nelle A. Curry of Grand Rapids, whose efforts won for her a University of Michigan Hopwood writing award in 1951, and who, after Constance Rourke's death, lived for a time with Constance's mother. I am grateful for all of Mrs. Butler's kind help, and grateful for being permitted to use the two biographical articles.

Thanks also go to my two sons, Joel Ethan and Jonathan David, for a wonderful Father's Day present in 1972: a copy of Rourke's *Audubon*, which they chanced to find in a small, out-of-the-way bookstore.

I am also grateful to Harcourt Brace Jovanovich, Inc. for permission to quote from Rourke's published works. Excerpts from Constance Rourke's *American Humor, Audubon, Charles Sheeler, Roots of American Culture, Troupers of the Gold Coast, Trumpets of Jubilee*, and *Davy Crockett* are reprinted by permission of Harcourt Brace Jovanovich, Inc.; copyright 1927, 1928, 1931, 1934, 1936, 1938, 1942 by Harcourt Brace Jovanovich, Inc.; copyright 1955, 1956, 1959, 1962, 1964, 1966, 1970 by Alice D. Fore.

Last but by no means least I wish to include a special note of thanks to my editor, Professor Kenneth Eble, for his rigorous, no-

Acknowledgments

nonsense approach to the craft of biographical writing and (by extension) to the art of pitfall-avoidance. I do appreciate all of his positive and helpful efforts.

Chronology

1885   Born November 14 in Cleveland, Ohio; daughter of Henry B. Rourke, a "hardware specialties" designer, and Elizabeth [Constance] Davis Rourke, a schoolteacher.

1888   Taken by her mother to live in Grand Rapids, Michigan, to be her home for the rest of her life. About this time her father dies, having spent the previous two years in a tuberculosis resort.

1890s– Attends public schools in Grand Rapids.
1903

1907   Receives B.A. from Vassar College. Awarded the William Borden Fellowship for Foreign Travel and Study.

1907– Teaches grammar school in Grand Rapids.
1908

1908– Goes to Europe with her mother, with whom she remains closely associated. Studies at the Sorbonne in Paris.
1910   "Reader in the Bibliothèque Nationale and the British Museum." Following period of study in Paris and London, returns to the United States.

1910– Teaches English at Vassar. Gives up teaching to devote her
1915   time to writing. First article published (October 1915): "The Rationale of Punctuation." Suffers a serious illness which makes her a semiinvalid for the next few years.

1918   Begins to publish essays, book reviews, and commentaries on the American cultural scene in a variety of periodicals: *New Republic, Freeman, Nation, Saturday Review of Literature, New York Herald Tribune Books*, etc.

1921   Publishes two fictional sketches in the *Dial*: "The Porch" (October) and "Portrait of a Young Woman" (November).

1924   At the MacDowell Colony for artists, in Peterborough, New Hampshire.

1927   *Trumpets of Jubilee*, a series of biographical studies of Henry Ward Beecher, Harriet Beecher Stowe, Lyman Beecher, Horace Greeley, and P. T. Barnum.

1928   *Troupers of the Gold Coast or the rise of Lotta Crabtree*, a biography of the once-famous performer, and a treatment of theatrical life in the greater San Francisco area in the later nineteenth century.

1929   Spends five months in England—in Torquay, Devon—working on *American Humor*, research for which will take her all over the United States.

1930   Again at the MacDowell Colony.

1931   *American Humor: A Study of the National Character*, a philosophical analysis, filled with striking examples.

1934   Serves as a national committee member for the First National Folk Festival in St. Louis, Missouri (April 30–May 4). *Davy Crockett*, a fanciful biography intended for young readers.

1936   *Audubon*, an imaginative biography.

1937   Editor of the *Index of American Design* of the Federal Art Project.

1938   *Charles Sheeler: Artist in the American Tradition*, an informal biography making extensive use of the artist's direct statements.

1940   Active in the Grand Rapids chapter of the Committee to Defend America by Aiding Britain.

1941   Dies, March 23, as a result of a fractured vertebra from a fall on the ice the week before. Funeral held in the East Congregational Church in Grand Rapids, March 26. Burial in Woodlawn Cemetery.

1942   *"The Roots of American Culture" and Other Essays* published posthumously with a preface by Van Wyck Brooks.

CHAPTER 1

Vignettes and Cameos

I Her Town: Grand Rapids, Michigan

TWO brief epistolary comments, each containing a kernel of psycho-geographical significance: the first is dated February 21, 1927, from Long Island City, New York. The young Lewis Mumford, fairly launched on his career as an architectural critic-historian and cultural commentator, writing to the eminent literary critic Van Wyck Brooks (shortly before Brooks's severe mental breakdown): "Constance Mayfield Rourke had just the sort of thing we should have liked [for *The American Caravan*, their "yearbook of new American writing"]; but Harcourt is bringing it out this spring. (She is a dear, by the bye: she, and she alone, saved me from the lowest depths of boredom in Grand Rapids: we got on famously, for I discovered early in our acquaintance that she had a deep respect for you.)"[1]

The second is dated March 5, 1930, from Worcester, Massachusetts. Constance Rourke, writing to Mrs. Linda Butler back in Grand Rapids: "Your valentine handkerchief is very charming, and it was very sweet of you to send it, with the pretty little heart. I christened it at a most lovely Concert last Sunday afternoon, one of those put on by a friend of mine here in a hotel ballroom, much like the Pantlind only better acoustics. The concerts are most wonderful & I wish someone would do the same thing in G. R. Life would be bigger and better."[2]

Having spent most of her active life in Grand Rapids, Constance Rourke we may assume was influenced by it and let its character creep into her work. What did such a town, so drab and ordinary on the surface, have to offer this lady? She was, after all, to write about the expressions of the artistic impulse that came from the people in communities like Grand Rapids, and that now and then would be rendered in imposing terms by a gifted artist. What was there in the town to nourish her spirit? In order to attempt an answer I shall first say something about the history, topography, and socioeconomic background of Grand Rapids.

In 1826 a trader named Louis Campau visited the area now occupied by the town. It was the site of an Ottawa Indian village on the rapids of the Grand River about thirty miles from Lake Michigan on the west, where a number of Ottawa Indian trails came together. Campau, surveying the scene, reasoned that this would be a good place for commerce with the Indians. Accordingly, not long afterward he founded Grand Rapids as a trading post, and the latter, now a branch of the American Fur Company, was incorporated as a village twelve years after his arrival. In 1850 it was incorporated as a city.

Two factors promoted the development of Grand Rapids as a major center of lumber processing and woodworking. The Grand River in this region, with its eighteen-foot fall, provided an excellent source of water power. And the surrounding forests of pine and hardwood (mahogany, oak, maple, etc.) yielded an abundant supply of lumber. Sawmills and woodworking enterprises multiplied. By the later 1870s, following the 1876 Philadelphia Centennial—at which furniture manufactured here was put on display—furniture buyers from all over the United States (thirty-eight states had been admitted to the Union by 1876) and in fact the world came to the Grand Rapids furniture markets. Skilled artisans and craftsmen in the various branches of woodworking and cabinetmaking maintained high standards of excellence, and for many decades the city was regarded as America's furniture capital. Utilitarian as many of the pieces were, artful designs and styles sustained the distinguished reputation of the Grand Rapids product. World War I brought about a shift in emphasis, in the direction of metal trades, and over the next six decades the "diversification of industry" greatly reduced the importance of furniture manufacture and design.[3]

The population of Grand Rapids, which stood at 168,592 in 1930, 164,292 in 1940, and 197,649 in 1970,[4] has traditionally been drawn from many countries of Europe and from Canada. The Netherlands in particular has over the years contributed large numbers of settlers; Holland, Michigan is only about twenty-five miles away. Grand Rapids has a well-known Art Museum and an art gallery as well as a fine public museum (featuring, among other exhibits, a costume section and an extensive furniture section) and other cultural institutions. In ethnic terms, the town's "rich cultural mix" has probably had a good deal to do with the refinement of arts and crafts there, and the strong local interest in them. One begins to appreciate Constance Rourke's deep attachment to her community, an attachment that was well known to her fellow residents, many of whom paid eloquent tribute to her on her death.

Many residents of Grand Rapids have brought it fame. To speak of politics for a moment, this longtime Republican stronghold produced at least two famous Republican leaders: Arthur Vandenberg, who served in the U.S. Senate from 1928 to 1951, and Gerald Ford. Unlike Vandenberg, Ford was not born in Grand Rapids but was taken there as an infant. Ford won election to the U.S. House of Representatives in 1948, was elected House minority leader in 1965, was nominated for the vice-presidency by President Nixon in 1973 (the nomination was confirmed),[5] and succeeded to the presidency in 1974. All of which is interesting from the standpoint of Constance Rourke's own political commitments. She was a lifelong Democrat, but this does not seem to have affected her relations with her fellow townspeople, nor from all the evidence did it make her feel she was languishing within a disliked minority.

Grand Rapids produced a number of individuals who distinguished themselves in the arts. Leo Sowerby, a native son who remained in Grand Rapids until the age of fourteen, was a noted composer of religious music and received a Pulitzer Prize for his work in 1944. Spencer Tracy and Dean Jaggers began their acting careers with Grand Rapids' Wright Players in the 1920s. Among the important local painters were Mathias Alten, Gerrit A. Beneker, and Kreigh Collins. The famous White family of Grand Rapids included Stewart Edward White—noted for his novels of Michigan and the Old Southwest, the violinist Roderick White, and the painter Gilbert White.[6]

An article, "GR Makes Its Mark in the World of Books," by Doris Branson, in the August 9, 1964, issue of the *Grand Rapids Press*, describes the very many writers coming from the town and nearby communities. In addition to Stewart Edward White—credited with the authorship of fifty books—another important literary figure is mentioned: Arnold Gingrich, a 1921 graduate of Central High School, who founded *Esquire* magazine in 1933 and later became its publisher. Gingrich's novel, *Cast Down the Laurel* (1934), had a Grand Rapids setting and apparently angered many of the local people. Of Constance Rourke, the article states that "During her lifetime [she] had the distinction of 'never receiving a rejection slip.'" One of the better-known Grand Rapids writers who emerged after Rourke's time is Robie Macauley, author of the very controversial novel, *The Disguises of Love* (1947), and a short-story collection, *The End of Pity* (1957). From the editorship of the *Kenyon Review*, Macauley went on to assume the fiction editorship of *Playboy*.

There is no question that Constance Rourke was very much "at ease in Zion," at home in Grand Rapids, particularly since there was ample opportunity to participate in local art activities. In the 1930s, for example, she was a judge at the American Folk Art Festival—working with her close friend Mrs. William Butler, whom she assisted at the time that the Friends of American Art put on its first National American Art Show in the city's Art Gallery.[7] The clearest statement of her attitude toward life in Grand Rapids is probably to be found in one of her journalistic pieces, "Art in Our Town," printed in the *Nation* a year before her death.

"Our town" apparently is symbolic language for Grand Rapids. The article opens with an account of a young Dutch painter from Delft named Marinus Harting, who in 1854 made his way to a small Michigan village "that had been established as a trading post less than twenty years before," founded by a French trader and other French folk. (Michigan had become a state in 1837.) Harting, a product of the "'little' masters" tradition, copied daguerreotypes, painted pictures suggesting certain Dutch towns, and taught young ladies how to sketch. He had come there originally at the urging of a Calvinist minister of a large Dutch colony settled on the Lake Michigan shore.

There was a well-established belief, which Rourke would oppose, that art was of negligible importance on the American frontier, that the Dutch Calvinists and Puritan New Englanders frowned on artistic expression. The example of Marinus Harting must argue against such a view. Moreover, there were others like him, there were itinerant painters some of whose "highly individualized portraits" were "interestingly abstract and even modern." Pictures were brought in by settlers; nearby Pennsylvania Germans went in for water colors and portrait painting. As for some of the other arts, "music was to be heard everywhere in an abundance of old songs" with accompanying strings of various types, and from the outset "the cluster of villages roundabout had a strong literary flavor." Many other communities like "our town" had comparable influences, "and the arts had some sort of place in all of them."[8]

But what, Rourke asked rhetorically, remained of the arts when our country became increasingly industrialized in the course of the nineteenth century? Since she disagreed with such negative critics as Van Wyck Brooks, who argued that the American environment had a deleterious effect on American artists, she would be eager to refute the stock answer to the above question. This stock answer, in her words, was that "not only in the frontier period but in succeeding decades life in our smaller towns and cities has been too meager to give the artist nourishment. Aesthetic roots sent down there were bound to shrivel."[9] Her own contrary view was this. As the nineteenth century moved along, "our town" showed a diversified artistic response: Gothicism in the furniture of the 1870s and 1880s; what was called "Steamboat Gothic" in architecture; houses reflecting the classic tradition in an austere application. The town was spared an industrial boom and the concomitant urban blight. Nature's very self was incorporated as the town extended its borders to enclose such pastoral elements as farms, fruit-bearing trees, and rural gardens. Businessmen returning from Chicago brought back paintings reflecting that familiar urban yearning for the country. Original paintings had always been available for purchase here. By the end of the century the town had an entrenched artist who was able to support himself by selling his paintings. What is more, an important avant-garde art exhibition was held.

At the present time, Rourke continued, reminding the reader of the harsh decade (i.e., the Depression period) that had just ended, art instruction is flourishing in the public schools. "Our town," which has always had a goodly number of "Sunday painters," now has its eager young painters who work on Saturdays, and even a group of artists who are young professionals, some of them displaying individualism and impressive technical ability. What was taken as "the revolt from the village" a quarter century earlier seems to have yielded to a tendency toward a kind of *return*, and a number of these local artists show a measure of promise. In her fairly cheerful conclusion, Rourke included a mild caveat. The stay-at-home artist will face many problems. The medium he employs may not provide him with a "tradition" upon which to draw. The artist in "our town," say, may not take Marinus Harting as his master. But possibly he will discover "a more substantial American past in the arts" and more extensive "social continuities" essential to the artist, than he has looked for. It may even be that his creative powers are evoked by the "variations" to be found in the smaller communities.[10]

Whether or not the title of Rourke's 1940 article, "Art in Our Town," deliberately echoed the title of Thornton Wilder's 1938 play *Our Town*, she depicted (as he had also) a small, idealized American community. Much in her version of "our town"—for example, origins, geography, developmental pattern, artistic expression in the townspeople—suggests Grand Rapids, as I have surmised earlier. And this imaginatively reconstructed town, about which she wrote with such a strong sense of identification, contained the elements she would never tire of extolling (sometimes in subtle fashion) as prerequisites for viable American art. These were: a wholesome society composed of stable yet heterogeneous common folk, a sense of community, a harmonious relationship between inhabitants and environment, and abundant sources of cultural tradition to nourish the would-be artist and artisan.

Rourke's artistic creed, so closely bound up with her attachment to Grand Rapids, also owed—as the above indicates—a great deal to the eighteenth-century German cultural philosopher, Johann Gottfried von Herder. He had taught that a particular society's relatively few productions of fine art or great art were attributable not so much to distinctive artistic geniuses, as to the rich body of folk art developed by the society at large. Reading Rourke's cultural studies gives one a keen sense of what she felt were American art forms' genesis, location, and distribution. She does not let the reader forget the importance to American art of region, community, and democratic diffusion. Something she wrote in 1933, on American geographical divisions and the errors of Marxist criticism, reveals her Herderian artistic philosophy as applied to another art medium than that of painting: literature. "All literatures," she said, "have been based upon the slow accretions of folk elements. Through these a common medium is finally established—a language with commonly understood overtones and subtle implications, and also those broad distinctive underlying patterns of thought and feeling which at last make for form."[11]

Whether or not this might add significantly to our understanding of the art works (touched on earlier) emanating from Grand Rapids and its environs, it is emblematic of Rourke's own strong sense of where she was rooted. Throughout her career as a cultural historian and commentator she would extend such an awareness to include the entire American community: common folk, craftsmen, and artisans, and all levels of gifted artists.

II   *Her Life*

Constance Rourke's mother, the shaping force of her life, was born Elizabeth Davis—daughter of Joseph Bonaparte Davis (a Welshman) and Phoebe Angeline Mayfield (Davis)—in 1852, in the southern Illinois village of De Soto. The Davises had originally come from Tennessee and Kentucky. Joseph Davis was primarily a landowner on a fairly large scale, but as a lay preacher he also conducted revivals. For reasons that remain obscure, Elizabeth would have none of her father's religion. Rebelling against the authority that it represented, and that her father as well as her older brother (whose bossiness was to her unendurable) represented, she showed herself to be a fiercely independent spirit; she would remain such for the rest of her life.

Well educated for a young lady of her day, Elizabeth—who decided that she wanted to be named Constance and changed her name accordingly—later became a schoolteacher, pioneering in kindergarten instruction and progressive education. Oddly enough, and—again—for obscure reasons, her personality was markedly out of keeping with what it should have been, considering her professional commitments. For twenty years she was to be a school principal: harsh, rigid in the extreme, and not well liked. Owing to her father's effect on her, she would have no part of formal religion; when her own daughter Constance was growing up, she saw to it that the child had no religious instruction.

The younger Constance Rourke's father, Henry B. Rourke, met his future wife in St. Louis, where she had been teaching kindergarten after having been trained in Chicago and having taught there as well. Little is known of Mr. Rourke except a few significant facts. He had come to the United States, alone, from southern Ireland; the rest of his family would remain behind. Although born a Roman Catholic, Rourke had given up his religion. His occupation was designing "hardware specialties":

fancy lighting and door fixtures. The Rourkes did not remain in any one place for very long, but as they moved about Elizabeth was nevertheless able to do a certain amount of studying: painting, modeling, metal work. The couple was happy and enjoyed their relatively carefree existence. Their daughter Constance was born in Cleveland in 1885.

The next phase of the Rourkes' family life wears the aspect of a nineteenth-century American tragedy. Mr. Rourke was stricken with tuberculosis. When young Constance was one year old he was obliged to go to a resort in Colorado in order to improve his health. Lacking the medical facilities we take for granted in the 1980s (X-rays, vaccines, antibiotics, etc.), the resort for tuberculosis victims was not able to alleviate his condition; a year or two after being admitted, Mr. Rourke died. Now Elizabeth (Constance) Rourke would have to make her way unaided, teaching school, caring for her very young daughter, planning for an unprotected future. Although direct references to her father are hardly to be found in her published writings, Constance Rourke was taught by her mother to cherish his memory, and it was clear that she regretted his loss. Her mother never married again, and the two of them were to remain unusually close until the daughter's death in March of 1941. Mrs. Rourke, whose very reason for being had thus been removed, lingered on a few years longer and died on Christmas Eve of 1944.[12]

It is neccessary now to turn back to the latter part of the nineteenth century. Mrs. Rourke's lifelong concern, aside from the welfare of her beloved daughter, was early childhood education, as I indicated earlier. In an individualistic way she was an adherent of the progressive education movement, particularly as it related to kindergarten. In fact, a good deal of her educational philosophy derived from an earlier source, the nineteenth-century educational innovator Friedrich Froebel, who had introduced the kindergarten system. However, since progressive education (to say nothing of its predecessors) was so important to her—and, through her rigorous application, to her daughter—it will be helpful to underscore a few salient facts about this controversial movement.

Progressive education was intended to revolutionize the existing educational systems under which pupils were supposed to be molded and programed according to some official authority's inflexible set of principles. In his historical survey, *The Transfor-*

mation of the School, Lawrence Cremin observes that "progressive education began as part of a vast humanitarian effort to apply the promise of American life—the ideal of government by, of, and for the people—to the . . . urban-industrial civilization that came into being" in the later 1800s. So to say, "progressive education began as Progressivism in education: a many-sided effort to use the schools to improve the lives of individuals."[13] The principles of this new philosophy involved among other things encouraging the child's personal growth through enrichment of his experience, and providing for the child a wholesome educational environment free enough from constraints for him to realize his powers and capabilities. One point in particular, according to Cremin's overview, is highly suggestive for our study of Constance Rourke's career as a historian-commentator working with popular American art forms. "Progressivism [in education], " says Cremin, "implied the radical faith that culture could be democratized without being vulgarized, the faith that everyone could share not only in the benefits of the new sciences but in the pursuit of the arts as well."[14]

Taking all of this into account, it is curious that young Constance would grow up in relative social isolation—even though she was the only child of an ill-tempered, widowed mother living on a slender income and having no other close relatives nearby. A lady who knew the family, Miss Nelle Curry, speaks of Rourke's failure to become friendly either with the wealthy sorority types or with the laboring-class independents, while in high school, though she did belong to two associations: the literary society and the basketball club. That seems to have counted for little, particularly since Rourke was unable to do any real entertaining and since her strong opinions—derived in some way from her mother—annoyed a number of the other girls.

One is tempted to speculate that Mrs. Rourke, for all her adherence to the ideals of progressive education and its kindred philosophies, was the victim of some "imp of the perverse" and could barely help belying those ideals with her irritating and antagonistic personality. Perhaps the explanation is not that simple. It might have been that the mother strove not wisely but too well, to advance her daughter's education. Miss Curry puts it this way, in speaking of the two Rourke ladies' profound attachment to each other. Mrs. Rourke dominated young Constance "as a child . . . by affection and drive," possibly with good results, for the most part. This domination brought about "a loneliness and aloofness that might have been sad" were it not "for college." Determining "that her daughter's gifts should be developed and focused," Mrs. Rourke "gave her daughter what was a later 'progressive' education [*sic*] at home, though it entirely lacked the social importance of the 'progressive' education of today [i.e., 1951]."

Upon graduation from high school, the young Rourke did additional work in English with one of the teachers there, and a year later entered Vassar, as she had earlier planned to do. The class prophecy saw her attending this prestigious college for ladies, saw her in fact capturing many young men with her "brilliant wit," and finally marrying "a well known man from Harvard."[15] Little information is available on her Vassar years. She received her bachelor of arts degree in 1907. Apparently, though, she had done quite well in her studies, for she was awarded the William Borden Fellowship for Foreign Travel and Study; in order to qualify she was required to have completed two years of English and two years of economics. But at this point there was another hiatus. She did not go abroad right away but instead devoted the next year to teaching the primary grades back home in Grand Rapids.

In the fall of 1908 she went to Europe, accompanied by her mother, and spent most of the next fifteen months in the two great capitals, London and Paris. In London she read at the British Museum and in Paris she worked at the Bibliothèque Nationale, studied at the Sorbonne, and became acquainted with the work of the modern painters: impressionists and postimpressionists. But her primary interest and career plans at this time apparently involved education. On her return from Europe in 1910 she wrote an extensive report for the Borden Fund on her research. In England she had studied methods and curricula in education, in addition to investigating "social movements" of the time and attending lectures given by Sydney Webb and J. A. Hobson. There was another scholarly pursuit, involving literary criticism and having some possible application to classroom instruction; it concerned the "psychology of narrative," and she was particularly interested in narrative because she felt that it figured so prominently in the elementary school curriculum.

Now, back in the states, she embarked upon a teaching career at her alma mater, Vassar, where she was to remain until 1915.[16] A fiftieth anniversary celebration was held in October of that year, and as chronicler of the event, Rourke in her remarks reflected the characteristic optimism and the sense of community, as well as the occasional flabby generalizing, that marked her prose observations. "'The celebration was an expression of the will and energy of a united community . . . If the success of the experiment involved in the founding of the college were in need of proof, surely that proof would exist in the ease and confidence, the pleasure and zest, with which the college of today, now grown to a full sense of power, united for creative effort, producing a celebration which was not only memorable in idea and purpose, but touched with beauty.'"[17]

In 1915 Constance Rourke, as indicated above, gave up teaching at Vassar and returned to Grand Rapids, where she would spend most of the rest of her life (traveling time excepted) living quietly with her mother, writing magazine pieces, book reviews, and a number of full-length studies of the American cultural scene. Teaching per se was not permanently abandoned; around 1919 she taught school briefly in the town,[18] and in later years shared her knowledge and expertise with others on an informal basis, and quite effectively. But, in 1915, there was this major vocational shift in her life, and the question is: what brought it about?

Several explanations have been given. First, she did not wish to devote her life or the major portion of her time to teaching;[19] she would prefer to write. Second, her mother, to whom she would always be very closely attached, had remained in Grand Rapids at her school post, and for Constance to establish herself permanently at Vassar, in faraway Poughkeepsie, New York, would mean that the two would see each other seldom, except during summer vacation. Mrs. Rourke was in her sixties; as time went on she would need more and more physical and emotional support, which only her daughter could provide.[20] Far more important, apparently, Constance suffered a serious illness at this time and was several years recovering from it; her mother helped nurse her back to health. The conventional view was that of a close friend of hers, Helen Balph, who wrote in a letter to Mrs. William Butler (the letter is undated) that Constance Rourke left Vassar in 1915 "because threatened with tuberculosis." Miss Nelle Curry, who lived for a time with Mrs. Rourke and was in a position to know, in her 1951 paper on the Rourkes found two causes of Constance

Rourke's debilitating illness. Tuberculosis was one. Mrs. Rourke
had always commented on the remarkable resemblance between
Constance and her dead father; even Mr. Rourke's "rich Irish
voice" seemed to have reappeared in her. Now the daughter had
contracted the father's disease too. But, after completing her
paper, Miss Curry found out from Constance Rourke's doctor *that
she had never suffered from tuberculosis:* her problem had been
heart trouble.[21]

The strong affection Rourke felt for American folk culture, for
our different modes and levels of artistic expression, must surely
have been fed by her deeply ingrained habit of traveling far and
wide to gather materials for her writings. She heard America
singing, telling homespun tales; saw America painting, making
domestic crafts; felt America's pulse as it obeyed its artistic
promptings. Commenting on her research habits, she once wrote
that when conditions permitted, she tried to know the area she
was writing about, "'and to learn at first hand the traditions from
earlier periods which still remain.'" She listened at length "'to old
timers in many parts of the country—old stagecoach drivers,
miners, actors, jig dancers, stage-managers, lumberjacks, river-
drivers, dulcimer players, ballad-singers, steamboat captains,
farmers, plantation owners, and other elderly people who never
had a vocation.'" She did this because she liked it. Although she
felt certain that much time was wasted doing all of this, she
believed it was "'essential if one is to write about American
traditions.'" Quite a number of "'current theories as to the
American character can be upset by this sort of unplotted discussion.'"[22]

Similarly, a biographical profile in a librarians' periodical, after
the publication of her *Audubon* (1936), touched on her "'living
research,'" which necessitated her visiting "all parts of the country. She has known old-time lumberjacks in Michigan and listened
to their songs and stories. She has talked with old minstrels,
vaudeville actors, theatrical managers, stage coach drivers, and
miners in the West, and with mountaineers in many parts of the
country. With their help she has tracked down old ballads, songs,
stories, and folktales, and made them a part of our written literary
history."[23] As early as 1931—when her magnum opus *American
Humor* was published—she was known as a seasoned traveler.
Local newspaper accounts at the time detailed her journeyings.
The *Grand Rapids Herald* on November 13, 1931, devoted a good

deal of space to her books and writing habits, concluding with a
note on her most recent movements. She was then on a trip to the
East, intending "to give two lectures on literary topics connected
with her field of research at each of the following places: Vassar
college, Bennet school, New York university, and the National Arts
club." She had been "a speaker on the program of the Michigan
Library association" that fall and had "recently lectured at
Western State Teachers' college."[24]

An account of a three-week summer auto trip taken by Rourke
with her close friend Margaret Marshall in 1938 is given in the
latter's unpublished paper, "Constance Rourke," to which I have
referred earlier. They drove through New England, vacationing in
a leisurely fashion, but Rourke "as usual, was gathering material
and noting it on the little blue slips she always carried." At this
time she was trying to find a number of artifacts, among them
"anonymous wall paintings," and succeeded in locating several
around Connecticut. In Maine and New Hampshire they visited
Shaker colonies. Only a few Shakers were now to be found "in
each colony, all of them elderly except for one young woman of
intact faith and clear intelligence." They visited many museums
and, if Marshall remembered correctly, on their return they went
to see the well-known painter Charles Sheeler—the subject of a
book by Rourke, published that year—and his extensive Shaker
furniture collection (in Pennsylvania, apparently).[25] Here as elsewhere Constance Rourke appears as the passive observer, enjoying
her findings and duly recording them, garnering fresh impressions
from her travels through rural America, where she might meet a
colorful variety of conservators of our native folk traditions.

From 1915 until her death in 1941 Constance Rourke published
two literary sketches and over a hundred journalistic pieces:
among them essays on many aspects of life in the United States,
book reviews on a wide variety of subjects—in such periodicals as
the *Dial*, the *New Republic*, the *Nation*, the *Freeman*, the
Saturday Review of Literature, the *New York Herald Tribune
Books*. Six books appeared during her lifetime: (1) *Trumpets of
Jubilee* (1927), biographical studies of Lyman Beecher, Harriet
Beecher Stowe, Henry Ward Beecher, Horace Greeley, and P.T.
Barnum; (2) *Troupers of the Gold Coast or the rise of Lotta
Crabtree* (1928); (3) *American Humor: A Study of the National
Character* (1931); (4) *Davy Crockett* (1934), and (5) *Audubon*
(1936)—two popular biographies for a teenage as well as adult

market; (6) *Charles Sheeler: Artist in the American Tradition*
(1938). In 1937 she served as editor of the *Index of American
Design* of the Federal Art Project. This was for her a sheer labor of
love, since the aim of this undertaking—to "provide the pictorial
records of objects that reveal American traditions in the useful and
decorative arts"[26]—was in line with one of her deepest concerns.
The year following Constance Rourke's death, 1942, a collection
of eight of her papers, six of them never before published, was
brought out under the title *The Roots of American Culture.* The
editor was Van Wyck Brooks, with whom she had earlier disagreed over America's ability to nourish and sustain its native
artists. The book represented some of the raw material of a long-
projected major work, a three-volume *History of American Culture.*

She never married. According to Miss Curry's paper on the
mother and daughter, when quite young Constance Rourke made
an odd statment on the subject of matrimony. She intended "to
marry, have a baby and get a divorce at thirty-five." Several men
did propose to her and she "broke off one engagement, probably
because of her basic individualism, love of freedom of action; also,
because of fear of danger to her work from domestic preoccupations." Both Rourke ladies were subject "to sudden, capricious
revulsions of feeling."[27] In the words of Mrs. William Butler, "The
great story behind Constance, I am sure, was the daughter-
mother relationship. . . . the whole inspiration Constance had to
write as she did was her mother. Her mother always read and
criticized her work before it was published. Constance realized
the enormous hardships her mother had, in giving her daughter
her education in the best schools possible."[28]

Kenneth S. Lynn, in his introduction to the Harbinger Edition
of *Trumpets of Jubilee,* suggested that the extreme closeness of the
two ladies had something of a baleful influence. He cited *Troupers
of the Gold Coast or the rise of Lotta Crabtree* as an indication of
this. Constance was attracted to the career of Lotta Crabtree, he
opined, partly "because of the touching, lifelong intimacy between an artistic daughter who never married and her mother, a
relationship that bears a strong similarity to Constance Rourke's
relationship with her mother." Two of Rourke's books, *Trumpets of
Jubilee* and *American Humor, are* dedicated to her mother, as
Lynn pointed out, but they represent only one third of the books
she might have dedicated to her. To italicize his point, however,

Lynn quoted from *Troupers of the Gold Coast* and added a speculative comment: "When she wrote that 'the bond between Lotta and her mother was close—too close, too confining, even mysterious, some observers said—but there was no sign that it chafed,' she might have been describing her own situation."[29]

Why did Lynn not quote further from the same passage on the same page? These comments by Rourke seem no less revealing: "Perhaps Lotta had been swept into her career by Mrs. Crabtree's will; her life in consequence may have been narrowed or cramped. Yet this choice had given her in abundance possibilities which she had deeply enjoyed." She "had remained young: her mother had grown old far before her time; she looked old, even at times deeply troubled."[30]

As Miss Curry discovered, the Rourke ladies were uncommunicative regarding trival personal matters. Constance's "literary friends" felt that in her case "it was a natural withdrawal, the reserve of any poet, painter, or writer," a protective device guarding her against people's demands and against "impressions crowding in too fast." But, she reasoned, the air of secrecy, of mystery, about the two was something special and was felt by those who knew the ladies. Much of this was due to the mother, who saw to it that Constance, like herself, did not speak to anybody about personal matters. Fiercely independent all of her life, Mrs. Rourke resented and rebuffed intrusions into her privacy, as for example after her daughter's death, when she felt that the government had no business appraising the estate, the real and personal property. Deeply suspicious of those who came within her purview, she seemed to ascribe base motives to all: visitors "wanted" something, the maid would steal, a friend staying with her had lied about where she had gone out.[31]

The point of all this is that Constance was affected in any number of ways by her mother's restrictive, hard-bitten personality. The outward sweetness of Constance's manner, her kindness and likability, the air of optimistic contentment that pervaded her writings, must be seen against a background containing a number of harsh, unpleasant influences to which she had managed to accommodate herself. There is the matter, for instance, of her political interests. A dedicated liberal Democrat in a conservative, isolationist town, she gave herself unstintingly to progressive and humanitarian causes. "She helped organize meetings for racial equality and civil rights," according to Miss Curry. Her efforts were also given to promoting greater public understanding of "the labor program" and to support our "program of aid for Britain"; the democratic cause "was her primary interest in life" and in her view our nation's democracy "had to begin and to be vital in the immediate community in which one lived." Ever the supporter and promoter of the arts, she helped organize a highly successful adjunct to the Grand Rapids Art Gallery, the Friends of American Art.[32]

One night, in March of 1941, she attended a public meeting called by the William Allen White Committee to Aid the Allies. "The friends who brought her home drove away as she went toward the steps of the porch. It was a wet night and a cold one— and the porch was icy. Constance slipped and fell. She knew she had hurt her back but she did not wish to disturb her mother, and she somehow made her way into the house and upstairs to her room."[33] When she was examined at the hospital the following day, the doctors discovered that one end of her vertebrae had been fractured. There appeared to be nothing very serious about this. For several days, after being treated, she continued to make a satisfactory recovery. Then, just as she was about to be discharged from the hospital, she collapsed—an embolism had formed. Shortly after, she was dead.[34]

Not long before, ironically enough, Constance Rourke had written to the editors of *Twentieth Century Authors* about her work, for inclusion in their biographical volume. Mentioning her "'living research,'" which involved going where the artifacts were, as well as the people who could talk about them, she added: "'If my work had meant only research in libraries, I don't believe I could have stayed with it, for as far as I can discover I am not a bookish person. When the day's work of whatever sort is done I turn not so much to books as to contemporary music, painting, the theatre, politics.'"[35]

Despite her mother's earlier attitude toward religion, Constance was given a traditional church burial. The funeral service was conducted by the Reverend Charles W. Helsley, pastor of Grand Rapids' East Congregational Church, and she was laid to rest in Woodlawn Cemetery. In his eulogy Reverend Helsley said, among other things, "'Constance Rourke as I knew her was the personification of the spirit of America at its best. She possessed a penetrating intelligence, wide range of acquaintances, an unusual appreciation of beauty and of art, a marvelous sense of humor and a rare human touch, the greatest of all the arts of life.'"

In a long tribute to Constance Rourke—printed like the above in the *Grand Rapids Press* after the funeral—Serrell Hillman, a young local man who had known her well (he was now a Harvard senior), praised her accomplishments, her modesty and kindness, her "'faith in the future of the middle west,'" and made this point about her feeling for young people. In his experience, the "'ability to identify herself thoroughly with modern youth [she] had to an unprecedented'" extent. "'Like a magnet, she gathered young people to her.'" He and his contemporaries "'who knew her well—never felt conscious of Miss Rourke's age.'" They "'never were embarrassed or confused in her presence. She was one of us, she grew with the times and remained always young in spirit.'"[36]

On the large grave marker in the family plot in Woodlawn Cemetery where mother and daughter lie in eternal rest, the following description is given of Constance Rourke's life and work: "American Biographer/Art Critic/Authority on Folklore."

CHAPTER 2

Recreating America: Journalistic Bits and Pieces

A great deal of Constance Rourke's literary effort was directed toward journalistic writing: essays, book reviews, sketches, topical notes, and the like; very early in her career she wrote a number of pieces on education and her alma mater, Vassar College. Rubin's *Constance Rourke and American Culture* includes a bibliography of around 130 items, published between October 1915 and the time of her death in March 1941; two posthumous listings are also given. The overwhelming majority of these entries are book reviews. Rourke reviewed fiction, poetry, children's reading matter, folklore materials, works dealing with popular arts and crafts as well as the fine arts, literary criticism, biographies, regional studies, and analyses of social issues.

While the reviews reflect her basic interests and concerns, just as do the longer and more important works, it will be more helpful I feel to concentrate on a limited number of her essays and sketches. Those I have chosen highlight many of the subjects that called up her deepest responses over the years. It is necessary first to mention what these quintessential subjects were, since they did so much to shape her entire writing career. They all relate to the American scene, the American experience in historical time and geographical space. Briefly, they are: (1) ars populi, that is, the various forms and kinds of art that are produced by the populace at large; (2) the world of the theater; (3) regional life in the continental United States; (4) American humor; (5) giants—things bigger than life; (6) the idea of community; (7) children's delights, that is, those extraspecial sources of diversion or entertainment that are particularly appealing to the very young. Clearly, a number of these subjects overlap or have extensive interconnections. The representative journalistic writings I shall take up fall into three categories: attempts at fiction, articles having to do with children, and what I shall call portraits of America.

I *Forays Into Fiction*

On rare occasions, Rourke tried her hand at fiction, or more accurately, the kind of journalistic sketch that merely crossed over into fiction. Her infrequent attempts here showed, among other things, a deep interest in various forms of popular art (and in serious art); escapist fantasies—in two of the pieces—that a child might conjure up; play-acting (not the same thing, in my view, as an *escapist* fantasy)—a "let's pretend" attitude toward life.

Three sketches in particular reveal Rourke's departure from the factual, reportorial, opinion-and-observation-based writing that she was accustomed to producing. In certain of her books, as Rubin observes, she would briefly attempt a storytelling, in fact, a mythmaking, mode of expression: in the opening of *American Humor*, for example. But in "The Porch" (*Dial*, October 1921), "Portrait of a Young Woman" (*Dial*, November 1921), and "Voltaire Combe" (*Nation*, October 7, 1939), Rourke was in each case inclined to tell a special kind of story of human challenge and response, holding the reader's attention with purely imaginative possibilities. Looked at in one way the two *Dial* sketches of young women are a little less representative of all her intellectual concerns than are the remaining journalistic pieces I shall speak of. But in another way they suggest much more about the inner, hidden Constance Rourke than any of the other writings could do, and for that reason are included here.

The mannered, self-conscious literary style of "The Porch" and "Portrait of a Young Woman" may well have owed something to the spirit of the times, modernism, in American literature and the other arts. Rourke, who had studied the impressionists and postimpressionists in Paris, now at the beginning of the 1920s had her own contacts with our Eastern artistic and intellectual centers of influence, and at the same time was well aware of the currents of change in morals and artistic standards. These two above-named experiments in the short-story form are actually pleas for a new, untrammeled way of life. They emphasize mood, atmo-sphere, image, domestic decor, and—in a seemingly personal way—unrealistic wish-fulfillment. Each sketch describes a young

woman who is (in effect) "stuck" at home with a single parent, but
is strong-willed, inclined to "do her own thing," interested in
travel and in getting away from where she is.

This in essence is what passes for a story line in "The Porch."
Maude Fassett, a vulgar, uneducated, irrepressibly wanton girl of
the lower middle class in a town which could conceivably be
Grand Rapids, was often away from home, gadding about in
automobiles with her raffish friends. Her father, whose name was
Henry—as had been the case with Constance Rourke's father—
was a traveling salesman who came home only twice a year for
brief visits; and her brother was also on the road, almost all of the
time. One day Maude "took off" with her creepy friends in their
motorcar, and did not return home. Writing to her mother from
California, Maude told her the original group had left but she was
staying on. She was in fact living with one or another of the men
she picked up there, and could not come back even if she wanted
to, because her mother was afraid of what the local gossips—who
were insatiably curious about Maude's carryings on—would say,
now. Henry Fassett, on one of his semiannual stopovers at home,
told his wife they should sell the house and she should move into a
flat. She refused, because she had begun to fix up her house (now
that Maude was gone for good) and had become quite attached to
it.

The escapist, wish-fulfillment feature of "The Porch" is fairly
clear. There is also the matter of "let's pretend"—the acting out by
the story's characters of artificial roles. For her mother's benefit,
Maude feigns a kind of surface respectability, while Mrs. Fassett
dissembles in vain to the local busybodies that Maude is merely a
high spirited girl; Henry Fassett, stonily indifferent to his family,
is only a shabby counterfeit of a husband and father. But not to be
overlooked is the theme of home decor. Rourke provided the
reader with details of Mrs. Fassett's and her neighbors' decorative
arts as applied to their porches; those porches, unlike the "un-
adorned" porches of the transient renters on "the small side street,"
all had "the same effect of decorative hospitality," shown through
their carpeting and their linen and cretonne coverings for the
porch furniture.

The point of the story, in fact, at least from Mrs. Fassett's
standpoint, seems to bear on home decor even more than on her
helplessness to do anything about her promiscuous, gallivanting
daughter. At the beginning, the Fassett porch was "fully if

somewhat shabbily furnished." But it was unused; both the mother and daughter, and Maude's wild friends driving up in motorcars, refused "the obvious invitation of the porch."[1] Only Henry Fassett, on his rare visits, would stroll up and down the porch. After Maude's departure, however, Mrs. Fassett suddenly took an active interest in fixing up her porch with new furnishings—to the point where Henry did not have much room to move around in. Moreover, the now-rejuvenated mother, thanks in part to the money Maude sent her, was also planning to renovate the interior of her house (as mentioned earlier). Only here, ironically, was the wife and mother at long last able to bestow her tender loving care. Her porch. Her little house.

There is no story line in "Portrait of a Young Woman." It is, literally, a verbal portrait of a nameless subject: the spoiled only daughter of a long-widowed manufacturing tycoon who has never remarried. Now, at age twenty-five or six, she is observed sitting and eating an ice, at the end of the dining-room table. Her personality traits are described in terms of paradoxes. She has an exotically tranquil air, and is always at war. Her affirmations are expressed as denials and her denials concealed as affirmations. Though she is not inclined to think ahead or retrospectively, and "her opinions are variable and contradictory"—never does she actually retreat. Though "malicious, she is also without guile." Bored by her father's friends, she will have none of them; yet, she enjoys debating the matter of those friends. "She is naive . . .[and] unapproachable."

Her father gives her an extravagant allowance, yet she tries to make her own clothes; he "is likely to exercise his rapid gift for satire upon them," yet she will justify the poor creations "always with her consistent negative undercurrent," admiring them out of reason, wearing them triumphantly as though anything she puts on will become her. As for the filial relationship, "Her most apparent bond with her father is a delight in fast driving." (Note: Constance Rourke did not drive.) She tears down the road, daredevil fashion, in her expensive motorcar. "When she drives she suggests that she might do something spectacular—from caprice—not with the car but with her own life"; she might run off with her auto mechanic or with a stunt flyer. Still, it does not seem likely she will soon marry, "though she has a knack which amounts almost to genius for picking up acquaintance with men, always by conventional but slightly circuitous, adventurous

methods." Most of these men, casual beaux at best, but with very
varied occupational backgrounds, are picturesque in some way,
and after playing with each for a brief spell she will set him aside.
All in all, the young woman's future does not appear dim by any
means: even with all her negatives she possesses "an elementary
capacity for happiness, something sudden and unexpected and
clear, like a waterfall in a dark forest."

Here again there is an unmistakable escapist, wish-fulfillment
element, in this sketch of a volatile, selectively gregarious, unpre-
dictable, fast-driving young woman, who may at any time decide
to leave her parent. What is fascinating is the way in which
Rourke combined the other two elements I mentioned, in regard
to her essays at fiction: play-acting— a "let's pretend" attitude
toward life, and a deep interest in forms of popular and serious
art.

This young woman has *created herself*, and the creation is
presented in terms that should easily have been understood by the
readers of 1921: a painting or drawing of a pretty, young woman
sitting pensively and provocatively against a colorful backdrop.
"Manet would have liked her short thick hands and the firm set of
her bust and hips," observed the author, but her subject suggests
the ladies in such poems as Wallace Stevens's "Sunday Morning"
and Ezra Pound's "Albatre"—both published a few years before
Rourke's "Portrait." Even more, her subject suggests the popular
art of magazine illustrations and pictorial advertisements of the
period: the stylized, alluringly posed young ladies (sometimes
shown without a colored background) of Charles Dana Gibson
and lesser artists like Neysa McMein, Anita Parkhurst, and
Harrison Fisher, to name only a few.

The sketch opens with a still-life projection of fruit in a large
bowl—"a reproduction of a late Renaissance piece" in the center
of the dining-room table. Supportive details suggest the author's
keen sensitivity to the nuances of interior decor, and her remarks
on the young woman's attempts to fashion her own wardrobe
indicate Constance Rourke's interest in another of the domestic
crafts. But she will be explicit in regard to her subject's strong
propensity to make over, to shape, her own material so that it
turns into *her own* imaginative and imaginary work of art.

At age sixteen, actually, this elusive charmer had begun "hesi-
tatingly, to create" that "long procession" of picturesque young
beaux—or friendly acquaintances. At the end of the sketch she is

reposing "in the long jade and gold drawing-room," and appears to reflect its glamor in her hair and her pale complexion; "she thrusts others out of the picture." That "drawing-room was her own idea; she regards it as a setting." But nature beggars art—the young woman's art, in the form of that very background she has created to set herself against: "her broad and subtle beauty shows the expensive decorations for the tawdry, flimsy, characterless things they are." She could if she chose strike out, shatter them, "and fling them to the wind."[2]

Maude's story, presented in the past tense, reads like a sordid daydream on the part of the author—a vision of freedom through wanton self-indulgence, expressed in words once and for all so that it might all the more readily be discarded. The young woman's "portrait," limned in the present tense, gives the impression of an eternally wished-for possibility: the author's alluring daydream of an alter ego that no familiar must be allowed to see—only distant, faceless, unknowable readers. Constance Rourke, according to Nelle Curry's study referred to earlier, "was fearful of psychoanalysis" just when so many were undergoing analysis.[3]

The third attempt at fiction, "Voltaire Combe," appeared in the October 7, 1939, issue of the *Nation* and was reprinted by Van Wyck Brooks in *The Roots of American Culture*, a collection of Rourke's pieces (some previously unpublished) on American cultural history, published the year after her death. "Voltaire Combe" stands somewhere between her two fictionalized sketches of modern, young, self-expressive American women, and her article "Art in Our Town," which describes an idealized midwestern community like Grand Rapids. This imaginative essay, which Stanley E. Hyman—in his Rourke chapter in *The Armed Vision* (1952)—mistook for a factual account, is a sensitive, knowledgeable commentary on the role of community and tradition in the shaping of the artist. It also provides a selective survey of fashions and modes in American art from the 1830s to the mid-1910s.

In brief, this fictionalized biographical sketch describes an American painter, who was born in a town called Jordan on the Erie Canal (i.e., between Albany and Buffalo) in 1837 and who died, a failure, in 1916. He was a youngster when he began drawing, and there was nothing unusual about this. "Limners freely plied their trade in and about Jordan" at this time. He admired this type of artist, and in fact the limners started him out on his career; they may also have given him "the idea that the artist was mainly the artisan, the honest journeyman." "His career," we find at the end of the sketch, "suggests that the impulse toward art may have had a wider spread in our nascent civilization than we have surmised."

In line with his artistic promptings, Combe created a new image of himself, a "let's pretend" image more romantic and colorful than his real self. "Like many of our earlier small-town characters he was something of an actor" and thus went on to affect "a pose and a vocabulary" far removed from his birthplace. Enlisting grandly—with his own fancy horse and sword and his dreams of glory—in the Union army at the start of the Civil War, he achieved the position of bugler and brought back from the fighting only sketchbooks "filled with pictures of himself in the thick of dramatic events." A few years after the war, in New York, Combe apparently produced pictures for the lithographers. He traveled along the eastern seaboard, developing a "courtly, persuasive manner."

Then he would return to Jordan for part of each year, painting the local characters—chosen "from homely and unprosperous levels"—in their typical attitudes, developing little village scenes somewhat in the manner of such genre painters as William Sidney Mount and Eastman Johnson. But with Combe, "character [was] foreground in all senses." Perhaps he did not understand the application of the media he used. At all events his village scenes and portraits showed close attention to physical detail in his "portrayal of character," though with an effect that was "sometimes labored, occasionally a little woolly." He began a long rambling novel, full of close physical detail; and he painted colorful characters from the literary classics.

Combe's pictures went unsold: they were not genteel enough, their painstaking detail was unfashionable. Impressionism, French art in general, were major forces in the art world, and Combe inveighed in vain against them, and against the kind of art exhibited at the New York Armory Show of 1913. Not that Combe was a great artist. Despite the emergence of the ashcan school of harsh urban realists years after Combe's own ungenteel pictures had been produced, he apparently had not exerted any influence on those who came after him.

There is something sad in Rourke's low-keyed rendition of Combe's life story. This early American artist, or artisan of the canvas and paintbrush, was divided against himself. In spite of his having come from the community of limners and having started working within their artistic tradition, his later development showed him to be isolated from other painters and out of touch with what was happening in the world of art. Esteeming the genteel, he self-contradictorily selected his subjects from the opposite walk of life, and his work was impeded because he did not have the vibrant contact "of others headed in the same direction."[4] So much for the "let's pretend" pose of the artist-artisan, so much for the widespread diffusion of the artistic impulse. Superior talent must count for something, after all, and so must keeping up with the times. "Voltaire Combe" is at once an impressionist view of recent American art history, a nod to Herder, and a cautionary tale.

II   *The Children's Corner*

Two magazine essays, for adult readers but having to do with children, are worth looking at here. Brimful of generalizations and theoretical assessments, they bespeak a teacher under the influence of progressive-education philosophy, a teacher who knows children only impersonally, as anonymous charges to be dealt with according to some approved formula. They reflect Miss Rourke's ideas about (1) America's common store of folk traditions and folk art; (2) a kinder-community which can find delight in individual expression as well as group effort; (3) the necessary limits—for artist or child or ordinary person—of conformity to the community norms. But for the reader to appreciate Rourke's particular approach to dealing with youngsters—whose outlook somewhat resembled hers, despite the psychic distance she maintained—and to appreciate also her mingled worries and more powerful optimistic flights of fancy, an interesting remark she made in a book review, in 1921, must be cited. Assessing two volumes of fairy tales and folk tales retold for children by Padraic Colum, she wrote: "The stories are a common possession because of their essential poetry and their supple telling; they have belonged to children first perhaps because children will more quickly take for granted a perfect and a simple world."[5]

In "Private Life for Children" (*New Republic*, August 10, 1921) we see a "fair field full of young folk" in a kind of dream-vision framework: they are faceless and utterly unreal. The article begins: "Responsibility seems to be the present watchword for the ordinary child—young child. He puts his small shoulder to the wheel of progress early." The article ends on a note of utter vagueness: "But the children themselves, with their perennial energy and curiosity, run (in crowds) expertly into one blind alley and out again and into another, picking up all the silly little slogans and rewards, following a lead or taking it, and leaving their youth behind them."

Early in the article Rourke gave the impression that something exciting, almost mysterious, was happening to the children of this new era, in the year 1921. (A brief historical note on recent events: World War I ended on November 11, 1918; the United States and Europe had been enduring a disastrous influenza pandemic; President Wilson failed to win approval for his peace treaty and League-of-Nations-Covenant proposals; Prohibition and Women's Suffrage went into effect [1919,1920]; Warren Harding became president in 1921.) One of the things the late war started, Rourke pointed out, was that it "showed the simple usefulness of children when they are consecrated to a cause." And in the name of that cause they made speeches and helped publicize our war effort in so many different ways as to throw open "the field for children's patriotic, social, and even cultural work." At present the children "are massed for action; and their stirring efforts are proceeding by leaps and bounds."

In a mild way this seems to hint at a kind of takeover of society by children acting under higher authority, something like what Ray Bradbury described in his sinister story, "Zero Hour." But this is not what happens in Rourke's curious article that attempts to capture the spirit of the times. The young folk of 1921, it appears, are simply being used by various agencies, as they are organized into effective little activity cadres or teams to further the Americanization movement and a variety of other kinds of programs. Various organizations get them "to rake leaves, can fruit and vegetables, run errands, visit the sick . . . there is an exact list of approved useful or noble acts which they are led to perform—for prizes." Given the enormous variety of interest groups available, practically every child can enter several of them and thereby advance other people's aims.

Rourke went on to complain about the regimentation of school children into health programs—with health duties and well-publicized rewards such as gold stars. And she extended her criticism to include (1) the American mother, who was forcing intensive doses of culture on her beleaguered child; and (2) the teachers (once again), who were pressuring the children with "the vocationalism which seeks to mortgage their futures." Before long the basic purpose of "Private Life for Children" begins to reveal itself. There is not a private life for them, but there should be. This rigid disciplining of school children into activity groups and ad hoc organizations worked against the general principles of progressive education, or of the educational philosophy of a reconstructed progressive like Mrs. Rourke. And, her mother's daughter, Constance Rourke would be likely to find such manipulating of youngsters extremely undesirable. In fact, she was speaking out against something else as well: children's peer-group pressure in the matter of clothes, hair styles, social manners, and the like.

Finally, Rourke seemed to be underscoring a basic point here, about the dismal effects of conformity by children, and the implications for our society. These young people, she felt, are in a good position to create "that homogeneous nation which is the dream of many of our patrioteers." (However, the incredibly small, atypical sample of children—white, comfortable middle class, midwestern—dealt with here, to judge from her remarks, seems never to have occurred to her.) Those patrioteers "are perfectly assured, if rather restless"; the teachers are uncertain—"as a substitute for faith they are heaping up works"; finally, "if their children have been caught in the current revels, their elders are rather more than bewildered; they are anxious."[6]

"Traditions For Young People," drawing on materials she had made use of in an address before the American Library Association in June 1937, was printed in the *Nation* the following November. Here she foresaw the possibility of a wonderful existence for all, through the means of art, group activity relating to the continuity of American tradition, and an up-to-date version of progressive education. Children, she suggested, might well be allowed to help in discovering the American cultural past, by finding and cataloging artifacts and works of art by forgotten craftsmen and artists. (She had in mind the work done recently by her Federal Art Project group in preparing the *Index of American Design.*) Her emphasis was not on practical application, through copying or adaptation. She wanted American youth to become steeped in the knowledge of American art forms of the past—

designs, painting, folk music, etc.—"without any immediate purpose." And she was speaking as a progressive (or neo-progressive) educator bent on motivating children to care about and to enjoy what is made available to them. Our cultural heritage is important, she felt, but American cultural subjects—art, literature, etc.—have been allowed to become "a dull duty."

In describing, in a general way, how young people might develop the properly realistic approach in dealing with folk art materials—say, folk heroes like Davy Crockett, Paul Bunyan, Mike Fink, and Pecos Bill—she took this position. A sense of what is real, in the present context, comes through a firsthand discovery of "materials in pristine forms," in a variety of fields, "so that a whole texture becomes apparent." Books are not the only means for retrieving the past, she pointed out, calling for special "American" rooms to be set aside in our libraries, where all available records in the practical, literary, and fine arts might be arranged together to help define a particular place and time. Here she struck a dominant note: tradition gave rise to the arts but their growth was slow, and this is a fact that educational planners and contemporary critics tend to forget.

All of which led her to a grand, utopian conclusion, a vision of a glorious, jubilant future, thanks to the little children, who might lead us. The youngsters are important because theirs "is an unconscious period, when many experiences may flow together without special purpose or thought, and wellsprings of the imagination be formed." If only these young folk could have full and easy access to the records of the American past, "with its poetry and homeliness, its occasional strange sparseness, its cruelties and dark failures," there might be "a great literature and music and art before we know it." Perhaps we will then "be able to devise equable ways of living." But at the least we might give young people "what we now possess, as fully as possible, with no strings tied."[7]

In this moving apocalyptic vision, the three modes of time come together in an explosive moment of wonderful possibility. We have the past with its roots of tradition—which are to develop into a luxuriant growth of variegated artistic splendor; the present, with its quality of an all-purpose, harmoniously functioning classroom; and the future, a golden age of all the arts and a societal utopia as well.

III   *American Sketches*

Constance Rourke's tentative efforts at fiction, like her articles on the life and activities of American children, highlighted certain features of her own life of the imagination: among them, the desirability of personal freedom of expression and movement, and the supreme importance of cultivating the arts—our cultural heritage. I shall discuss briefly four more of her journalistic pieces, "American sketches" taken from the *New Republic* and dating from the period between 1919 and 1936. All are expressive of various of her special interests, concerns which help define her distinctive approach to the American experience.

The first article, which appeared August 27, 1919, dealt with current stage-variety offerings and was titled "Vaudeville." From it we can gain an insight into how Rourke's mind worked when she was responding critically to a particular art form. And we can get some idea of her attitude toward the humor of professional entertainers. First, however, since she was always so enamored of the theater as a medium for live popular entertainment, a few remarks on vaudeville's history will be helpful.

Vaudeville came "out of the 'dime museums' of the late 1800's with their freaks and pickled fetuses, out of minstrel and medicine shows, its name somehow derived from the satiric *vau-de-vire* songs sung in the 15th century in Normandy's Valley of Vire." Since its inception vaudeville tried to present "'straight, clean, variety'—family fare—though the box-office lure of a sizzling Salome dancer tempted many an impresario." As the new century dawned B. F. Keith, one of American vaudeville's greatest pioneers, was booking "acts for 400 theaters east of Chicago; Martin Beck's Orpheum Circuit controlled two-a-days (matinee and evening shows) west to California."[8]

The period from 1910 to 1915 might be taken as vaudeville's Golden Age, and the medium "traditionally offered something for everyone." There was a mixture "of songs, dances, funny sayings, acrobats, animals, contortionists, illusionists, tightrope walkers, sketches, quartets, tenors, comedians," performing in two thousand theaters all over the country. The large cities boasted theaters of such major vaudeville chains as Keith-Albee, Orpheum, Pantages—but there were also "other theaters, offering [instead of two shows daily] three shows a day, or four, five, even six."[9] With this broad range of vaudeville offerings and frequently changing bills, there was a rich abundance of theatrical entertainment possibilities for the devotee to choose from.

In her commentary, Rourke was not concerned with small independent road-companies, but rather with big-time professional vaudeville, since the latter, for all its stifling effect on freshness and originality, had too much to offer to be seriously challenged by petty rivals. She was looking for something that vaudeville production numbers were sadly lacking—a single overall effect; generally there would be a disparity between action and setting. And she complained that the vaudeville medium did not maintain "any kind of level, much less its best, in the matter of settings." She was not calling for elaborately detailed backgrounds for brief skits: sometimes simplified settings would do quite well. However, "simplification of setting [was] no sweeping remedy. " What she objected to was the jarring incongruity of, for example, "a troupe of acrobatic dogs . . . set in a chalky grey imitation French drawing room, cluttered with pre-Mission parlor furniture," or "Burlesque dancing" in front of "the painted vast arcades of a porphyry palace or on the terraces of Lake Como." Even if the audience overlooked such discrepancies, the vaudeville number would still "fall short of its possibilities since it [lacked] the positive support which setting might give."

Rourke suggested ways in which setting might provide the necessary support: selective color-lighting for high-wire performers and stunt cyclists, a gay and beautiful "patchwork curtain" to serve as a backdrop for certain humorous routines, and so on. Further suggestions by Rourke stemmed from her remark— indirectly foreshadowing her editorial work on the *Index of American Design* in 1937—that the vaudeville acts requiring paraphernalia revealed an enormous "amount of decorative detail." Color, composition, and stage props such as playing cards and goldfish in bowls, were all to be considered for this kind of support. Such entertainment numbers as the girl locked in the trunk, the ducks pulled out of the sleeve or empty container, the mindreading stunt, could be enormously enhanced with the right kind of background.

In her conclusion she referred enthusiastically to the wide range of possibilities open to the vaudeville stage designer. Innovation and the introduction of the unexpected would always be necessary, but whatever daring changes were made in the settings, the latter "must not overshadow the performance" lest "the essentials of movement and active diversion" be lost. And at the very end she insisted that vaudeville needed always to suggest "comedy" or, failing that, a light mood; "humor in scenic effect is no small accomplishment."[10]

Though the "Vaudeville" article may not appeal to the general reader of the 1980s, it reveals among other things Rourke's highly developed sense of order: everything in its proper place. In this connection, if the artistic and aesthetic ideas in "Vaudeville" are examined more closely, two interesting connections may be seen with Gestalt psychology: the study of behavior, experience, perception, even a work of art on whatever level of taste, as dynamic wholes (i.e., as gestalts).

First, Rourke's complaint about incongruous settings for the vaudeville acts—actions—and her interest in deriving complete satisfaction from the effect of the whole performance, seem to relate historically to literary theory and practice as far as a holistic approach to the "work of art" is concerned. Aristotle's dictum in *The Poetics* about tragedy being "an imitation of an action that is whole and complete and of a certain magnitude," is an early instance of the art work, on whatever level of taste, popular or elite, being treated as a gestalt (even though the components of tragedy are described). The frequently contested three unities of time, place, and action, in drama over the centuries since Aristotle's time, represent a further instance. Lastly, there is Edgar Allan Poe's doctrine of the unity of effect—of impression—in a literary work. For her part, Constance Rourke was serious when she wrote of the frustration felt by the viewer when the vaudeville act was not, in effect, "together" because its two major elements were not in harmony.

Second, Gestalt psychology makes use of two important principles, "figure-ground" and "closure." According to the former, "perceptions are fundamentally patterned into . . . the figure, which stands out, has good contour, and gives the appearance of solidity or three-dimensionality; and . . . the ground, which is indistinct and whose parts are not clearly shaped or patterned." The closure principle has to do with organization of thought: "perception, memories, thinking—mental and behavioral processes in general—tend to completeness, good definition, and symmetry of form."[11] (Suggested examples: filling in the spaces in broken letters, straightening a crooked picture on the wall, wanting to change cacophony to euphony, etc.) In her "Vaude-ville" analysis, Miss Rourke felt that figure and ground should produce the best overall, unified effect—"comedy" or a light mood—and she protested that commercial vaudeville was not achieving this. In gestalt terms, the closure principle was being opposed. Though never using the term, she again invoked closure by calling for suitable stage decoration, proper scenic design with color, lighting, and stage setting: the myriad supportive elements necessary to realize an artistic vaudeville production.

From the magic, the excitement of the theater, to other of Rourke's deep loves: the concept of the superhero giant and the realm of folklore. "Paul Bunyon" appeared on July 7, 1920, and, as the title indicates, is about a famous folklore figure, reports of whose fabulous achievements seem to have intrigued her as much as the comic-strip adventures of Superman and Captain Marvel ever mesmerized a credulous child. (I shall use the more custom-ary spelling, Bunyan, unless I refer to the actual title.)

What she did in this article, which anticipates material in her *American Humor*, was to retell some of the lumberjack tall tales about the giant of the woods. To do this she made use of the folk materials collected by a forestry professor at the University of Michigan, P. S. Lovejoy, an authority on these geographically far-ranging accounts of Paul's size, strength, managerial ability, and general supernatural qualities. He could clear a vast expanse of timberland, feed a horde of his lumberjacks, plant a grain of corn that would shoot up sky-high while sending down roots that would reach under the Great Lakes, and so on ad infinitum.

Something deep in Constance Rourke's psyche must have been involved here in her recycling of these wonder-tales—which she would tell over and over, with heroes such as Davy Crockett, in later writings. Stanley Edgar Hyman, in his chapter, "Constance Rourke *and Folk Criticism*," in *The Armed Vision* (1952), made a cogent remark about the kind of raw material she was presenting here. The bulk of contemporary American folklore investigation, he felt, had "been preoccupied either with the aimless collection of folksongs, children's rhymes, and so forth, without any compre-hension of their significance or ability to sort them out, or with the retelling of such phony legends as the Paul Bunyan material for an audience on the juvenile level."[12]

Intellectually, this kind of tall-tale, presumably through associ-ation of ideas, harmonized with her notions of American humor.

But I believe that she actually recognized that the stories were ridiculous, and so her identification with their hero had to answer some hidden need. In her concluding statement in the Paul Bunyan article, she stressed the seeming indigenousness of "the rapid fertility and ingenuity of the stories" and "the zest with which situations are pushed to their furthest and their absurdity explored with a tireless patient logic." This led her to conclude that "the whole basic method of solemn, preposterous exaggeration touches the very core of American humor."[13]

On an emotional level, several explanations may be suggested for her interest in giant figures set against a diversified background, geographically and occupationally, of a developing nation. For one thing, it is possible that she retained viable memories of fairy tales read to her in childhood or that she herself read at an early age. The relish with which she related the anecdotes about Bunyan and other folk characters—Davy Crockett, for example, in her juvenile biography of him—suggests that she never outgrew them. There is another possibility, which may be drawn from a passage in Carl Jung's 1945 essay—based on a 1916 paper—"The Relations Between the Ego and the Unconscious." Constance Rourke had lost her father when she was very young. It is conceivable that what she heard about him over the years from her mother, who never remarried, acted on her mind in such a way as to magnify him out of all natural proportions so that his shadowy existence was transformed in her imagination to the superhuman size and wonder-working potency of a Paul Bunyan or someone like him. With the passage of time her long-dead father, whom she had practically never known in the flesh, might well have become her giant hero.[14] Nelle Curry, in her biographical paper on the Rourkes, reported that Constance's mother had very often noted the remarkable similarity between father and daughter: the latter possessed her father's "rich Irish voice." Miss Curry added that Constance had been "brought up to love" her father's memory and "spoke wistfully of his early death."[15]

Still one more possibility is available, again suggested by Jung's above-mentioned essay, this time from a section on the "mana personality." Jung wrote, "primitive man" neither analyzes nor works out just "why another is superior to him. If another is cleverer and stronger than he, then he has mana" and is more powerful, but that power may be lost if for example "someone has walked over him in his sleep, or stepped on his shadow. Historically, the mana-personality evolves into the hero and the godlike being, whose earthly form is the priest." It "is a dominant [*sic*] of the collective unconscious, the recognized archetype of the mighty man" seen as "hero, chief, magician, medicine-man, saint, the ruler of men and spirits, the friend of God." This figure has always been "in possession of the secret name, or of some esoteric knowledge, or has the prerogative of a special way of acting . . . it has an individual distinction."[16] Paul Bunyan, however legendary, is clearly a type of "mana-personality."

Some people are drawn naturally to such figures, in real life or in song and story. If the mana cannot by any means be expected to transfer over to them, they will still want to be close to it, hoping to realize residual benefits. At the least, writing about a "mana-personality" will give the writer some kind of identification with it. One might keep in mind Constance Rourke's deep fascination with Paul Bunyan the lumberjack giant, and with other giants in American folklore, as one considers this passage from Jung's treatment of the "mana-personality," which follows immediately the statement quoted above. No editorial comment is needed. According to Jung, "Conscious realization of" what makes up the "mana-personality" signifies, for a "man, the second and real liberation from the father, and, for [a] woman, liberation from the mother, and with it comes the first genuine sense of his or her true individuality."[17]

Next there is an interesting essay—dated September 20, 1933— on the shaping power of our geography, and such related topics as regionalism in literature, F. J. Turner's "significance of sections" hypothesis, and Marxist literary criticism. There is so much in Rourke's "The Significance of Sections" essay to consider that only a suggestive overview can be given. She made it plain that hers was an essentially populist view of art. Every literature, she argued, was based on "the slow accretions of folk elements," which would ultimately establish "a common medium" of language having generally "understood overtones and subtle implications, and also those broad distinctive underlying patterns of thought and feeling" that ultimately constitute form.

This is a very interesting remark within the framework of her "Significance of Sections" essay. The familiar reiteration of her trickle-up theory of art plays down the position of the imaginative, creative artist, making art now a collective process. What she did in the first part of her essay was to refute current Marxist criticism, which itself rejected the idea of regionalism in American life and its literature. Certain Marxist critics, V. F. Calverton in particular, had argued that the industrialization of our country had standardized and generalized our way of life—in labor, education, thought, culture,—to the point where it was no longer possible to think in terms of regions or sections. She on the other hand was all for geographical sectionalism as the basis for explaining our diverse folk-cultural heritage. And this led her into the position of appearing to express a belief in only one kind of populist art—the sectional—when another kind—the national or class-occupational—would be just as valid.

Constance Rourke, strangely enough, wanted it both ways. She (1) insisted on American cultural traditions deriving from the folk, who formed distinctive regional subgroups, and then (2) identified the folk with the transsectional proletariat (the Marxists' term for the poorest class of industrial wage earners): "the two have been pretty consistently identified in all countries." Her inconsistency or ambivalence in regard to just what kind of populist culture and art we have, is shown in this part of the essay. Enough of our folklore, she felt, had already been made available to show our "deeply rooted, widespread folk expression—regional in character, some of it quite explicitly proletarian in sentiment." Calverton, in discounting "the spirit of a region, its customs, folklore and native speech," thereby discards "a means of understanding (for purposes of revolution) our apparently standardized but deeply divided and enigmatic native life," ignores "the basis from which such a revolutionary literature can develop as he believes to be fundamental" and in addition suggests "that literatures are created by a miracle."[18] (Hence, the individual artist is considerably devalued.)

To emphasize a major aim of the essay: she wanted to refute the Marxist critics such as Calverton and Granville Hicks, whose view of American literature she found, in 1933, quite unacceptable. A good survey of Marxist theory applied to literary criticism may be found in the "Marxism and Literature" chapter in Edmund Wilson's *The Triple Thinkers* (1948) and the chapter on "Christopher Caudwell *and Marxist Criticism*" in S. E. Hyman's *The Armed Vision* (1952), as well as the section on Marxism in Rod W. Horton and Herbert W. Edwards's *Backgrounds of American Literary Thought* (1974). A brief note from Hyman is relevant: "the whole Marxist tradition . . . as a theory of interpreting society inextricably bound up with overthrowing it, sees all analysis in terms of present struggles and weapons."[19] Clearly this doctrinaire position would not have appealed to Constance Rourke.

Still, she conceded that the Marxist (Marx*ian* in her expression) ideas of Calverton and Hicks "cast a penetrating light across almost any group of writings," in fact, "any mass of material." Then she qualified this. "But so does any closely integrated theory concerned with human behavior: the Freudian theory accomplishes the same result for many readers." Now there followed a refutation of such theories. "The mistake is to consider that a literature—and perhaps a revolution—can take flight from an intellectual synthesis, and to ignore the humble influences of place and kinship and common emotion that accumulate through generations to shape and condition a distinctive native consciousness."[20]

To further rebut the Marxists (who held "that agrarianism is dead, overwhelmed by industrialism—completing the process of standardization"), and to advance her regionalist view of populist art, she cited Frederick J. Turner's recent book, *The Significance of Sections in American History,* which had won a Pulitzer Prize. Famous for his 1893 "frontier hypothesis," Turner now extended his philosophy of geographical determinism to sections. From the evidence he had accumulated he argued that the physical features of our various regions had directed where our different (ethnic) "stocks" would be located, and furthermore "that inherited customs, institutions and ways of looking at the world in the sections have continuously been shown in political life and popular opinion." He even advocated "'recognition of the geographic section as an integral part of the national machinery.'"

Rourke exemplified her belief that "social coherences" deriving from geographical regions are necessary for a great literature, by considering the genre of the novel. This form was "rooted in highly developed collective experience," in her view, and it has made its appearance in any literature "only after the nationalistic sense has become articulate, as racial identities [*sic*] have grown positive, as small social unities have been established, and groups have come to feel common bonds because of long settlement together or because of common fortunes."

Her discussion of the American novel founders between an attack on the Marxist critics and her own historical-collectivist bias. In her view our literature has been characterized by "chaos and scantiness." She considered only two legitimate forms of the novel, the novel of manners and the regional, folklore-laden novel; this position led her into very curious judgments. In her view the novelist of urban life still lacked sufficient localized social tradition for literary use; "Dreiser's struggle with style" symbolizes "effort against almost impossible odds," because he frequently "charted the large way of the novel through aspects of an urban life which had barely taken shape." William Dean Howells shared the same predicament with most novelists who followed him: "Chaos, uncertainty, incompletion . . . because of a widespread social incompletion." Not so, apparently, with certain regionalists drawing upon an ancient store of folk materials: Erskine Caldwell, Grace Lumpkin, Marjorie Kinnan Rawlings.

Fighting against standardization (a Marxist tenet) to the very last, Rourke cherished the lingering "stubborn variety" of colorful customs and artifacts associated with geographic pockets. She felt that we needed to conserve such traditions in their own sections so that creative works could continue to be produced. If this were not done, and we lost "what we have, we could become too deeply disintegrated as a people for natural expression and for any kind of social order."[21]

The last article to be considered here, "Artists on Relief," came out on July 15, 1936, and is as indicative of Rourke's essential core of belief as is any of the preceding examples. Here it is a matter of the populace and the artists it continued to yield up: two groups in which she reposed a great deal of admiring confidence. And she extended this "full-faith-and-credit" coverage to the benevolent and protective federal government, which worked (as she saw it) in various ways to improve the common lot—just as those other bodies, in their turn, were doing. The article reveals her strong belief that art could be handled, managed, promoted by government fiat-and-funding—that things would go well with us if only art were put on display and given a wide exposure among the masses. At this time the Great Depression, a debilitating blight, lay across our land. Her rosy optimism and intense faith in the future seem, in the 1980s, to have lent her the power of incantatory wish-fulfillment instead of a selective pesticide, to deal with that blight.

"Artists on Relief" begins by summing up the predicament of the beleaguered American artist up to the preceding year: 1935. Recently, according to Rourke, sculptors and painters have been told they should dig ditches; people wealthy enough to be "patrons of the arts" have come to adopt a "punitive attitude" toward American artists, who have occupied a marginal position in society, "favored neither by the rich buyers nor by the museums." True enough, "during the boom of the late twenties a fair number of fliers were taken in American art," but after the stock market crash of late 1929 our artists' "slight relations with a [*sic*] public were completely broken." A number of government agencies attempted to provide funds to encourage and reward the artists' efforts (one project, for example, involved "the decoration of public buildings"), but no agency "defined or met the many destructive forces at work or reckoned with the fact that a profound and permanent dislocation" in the history of American art might result. These agencies virtually neglected the predicament "of the young artist of distinguished but still emergent gifts."

Then came the month of August 1935, during which the Federal Art Project, a division of the Works Progress Administration (WPA), was established, and Holger Cahill was named its director. Constance Rourke had a particular reason for calling attention to Mr. Cahill's important new assignment, at a time when there were about four thousand artists on relief and, in addition, almost half that number "living on the margin of starvation."[22] He happened to be "our outstanding authority on folk art and American primitives," had been connected with the Museum of Modern Art in New York and New Jersey's Newark Museum, had organized "large municipal exhibitions," and—a writer and critic himself—was well versed in the history of American art.[23] Thus, Cahill's philosophy of art, as she explained it, neatly coincided with her own. She saw him as being "thoroughly acquainted with the relationship to the main streams of art borne by those minor and often anonymous artists whom we call folk artists" and thus as having "a working philosophy as to the conditions under which talent is brought into free expression."

What gave Rourke a great deal of satisfaction and pleasure was Cahill's bold, imaginative, expansive plan to integrate "the fine arts and the practical arts" as well as "the arts with the life of the community." Judging from her report, the plan was enormously successful. Among the varied and community-directed activities of Cahill's Federal Art Project (under whose auspices Rourke herself would serve as editor of the *Index of American Design* in 1937) were the following: preparing "maps and charts and large-scale relief maps, often of distinct beauty, . . . for schools and libraries"; providing "dioramas, lantern slides and settings for amateur plays" for local groups; designing posters for "health and safety campaigns"; making "scenic models of landscapes and figures of charm and interest . . . for museum exhibits" and exhibits of wild life; setting up "models of road building and other constructional activity"; and examining the uses of artists' materials so that their design may be improved.

And thus Rourke presented a very rosy view of government-funded *popular* art for the masses, as a relief measure (i.e., a means for putting unemployed "artists" to work) and as a basis for strengthening our nation through upgrading its cultural values. The Federal Art Project was planning to send exhibits of artists' work on tour, particularly to areas where the residents had not previously been exposed to formal art. Numerous classes promoting art appreciation were being conducted "for underprivileged children, taking them off the streets and providing fresh and natural outlets for expression."

Well aware, even less than a year after Cahill's Federal Art Project came into being, that noisy detractors would do what they could to undermine public confidence in our art-by-government programs, Rourke assured her readers that the several thousand artists "on relief" would "obviously. . . not produce masterpieces," but "that the artist of distinction and experience has been doing some of his best work for that abstraction called government." Instead of seeing this government sponsorship—with its internal politicking, favoritism, and capriciousness—as detrimental to the "artist" of high and low degree, she even suggested that their new freedom from outside commercial pressures, etc. would greatly benefit their work, and that the federal program for the arts would help young talent enormously.

Her emphasis, clearly, was not so much on the mainsprings of art, the inspiration that passeth understanding, as it was on the folk, who were regarded as a body of art appreciators and consumers, and also as the seedbed of art from which artists and artisans grow. She concluded by praising this new federal program, which had developed out of the idea that art was not the province of a few people merely—its place was in society at large, "for pleasure and use." Many problems would remain, for the artist and the "art movement": for example, "the salient one of making possible a wider possession of art by those who covet and need it." But much good might be expected from the program; among other things, "many new relationships" and the preservation "of permanent values," which the Great Depression had severely threatened.[24] The general idea of this last passage will come to have a familiar ring to the reader of Rourke's writings about artistic (or humorous) expression and its sources in the social group. Simply stated, the idea is this. Despite the progress that has already been made, many problems—or perhaps it is only one major problem—will still have to be solved; much work remains to be done.

By way of a postscript: the Federal Art Project, which was terminated in 1939 on a federal level, continued for a few years thereafter on the basis of sponsorship by individual states.

CHAPTER 3

Curtain Time and a Flourish of Trumpets: Five Entertaining Sketches

I *"Make a Joyful Noise"*

IN certain ways Constance Rourke's first book, *Trumpets of Jubilee* (1927), seems—in the 1980s—practically as important as her best-known work, *American Humor: A Study in the National Character* (1931). Often ponderous, like almost anything else she ever wrote, this thematic collection of biographical sketches is based on solid if carefully selected fact, and is developed according to a subtle contrapuntal design of dark and light, gloom and joyous hope. A number of the essential Rourkean objects of concern (art of the people, the world of the theater, regional life in America, American humor, giants and what they represent, the idea of community, children's delights) are touched on in one way or another.

But the book expresses with force, as earlier readers were doubtless aware, the dynamic quality of the American experience, perceived in historic and geographic terms. Moreover, her five subjects, four of whom lived entirely within the nineteenth century, gave her the opportunity to describe the American tradition in terms of breaks with our own more distant past as well as continuing links with that past. This additional dualistic quality, touched on in her epilogue, is presented through her concept of the need to "make a world out of a wilderness": the concern of young mid-nineteenth-century Americans, and (as she saw it) a necessity for Americans in the later 1920s. She also argued that such tokens from the earlier time as "magnitude," "largeness" of intention and action—which her subjects exemplified—would be a useful resource for contemporary folk.[1]

My aim in this chapter will be to introduce Rourke's biographical subjects, say something about what led to the trumpet-jubilation and the Calvinist depression that help structure her story, then continue to trace her chiaroscuro design as seen in those short biographies.

For her gallery of successful popular leaders representing what she called "the vicarious crowd," the author selected three members of the famous Beecher clan, noted for its Calvinistically oriented religious fervor (which time would somewhat dilute) and for its powerful preaching. First was the father, Lyman Beecher (1775–1863), the eminent and controversial Presbyterian minister of the Eastern seaboard, and president of Cincinnati's Lane Theological Seminary. Next, his daughter, Harriet Beecher Stowe (1811–1896): wife of the remarkably learned Bible scholar and linguist Calvin Stowe (1802–1886), and author of the immeasurably successful antislavery novel *Uncle Tom's Cabin*. After that, Lyman's son, Henry Ward Beecher (1813–1887), the spellbinding Congregational minister, later to be the principal in a notorious adultery trial. The other two figures were Horace Greeley (1811–1872), the renowned editor of the *New York Tribune* and advocate of the "Go West, young man" philosophy; and P. T. Barnum (1810–1891), America's greatest showman and impresario.

Despite her detailed account—derived from primary and secondary sources credited in a short postscript—Rourke was so highly selective that certain important matters are obscured or scanted. While there is a good deal of material on theological disputes and schisms within the Calvinist-oriented churches in the Eastern United States during the later 1700s and the following century, the discussion of Henry Ward Beecher's adultery trial and the preceding events is refined almost beyond the reader's understanding. The chapter on P. T. Barnum lacks the sparkle one would expect in a treatment of this rare sucker-baiter. And, a few preliminary notes about jubilee-trumpets, the millennium, Calvinism-Puritanism, and the making of all things new, would have rendered the material a little easier to follow. The ensuing brief remarks, in which I relate these theological and sociological matters to what I have called Rourke's "contrapuntal design," may be of some help at this point.

The jubilee-trumpets idea goes back to the biblical Hebrews and is mentioned several times in the Bible: Psalms 98:6 for example, and Leviticus 25. The latter discusses the Pentecostal jubilee year, following seven sabbaths of years. The trumpet shall sound throughout the land, and liberty shall be proclaimed unto all its inhabitants; slaves are to be freed, people are to regain the property they have forfeited, the land is to lie fallow and recover its fertility. However, the idea of this joyous recurring season, which had some appeal for Christian thinkers, was engulfed in two other time intervals, of far greater attraction.

The basis for these was a story near the end of the Bible, in Revelation 20–21. John the visionary saw Satan hurled into the bottomless pit and secured there for a thousand years. Those people who were saved by the witness of Jesus and the word of God were to live and reign with Christ for a thousand years—but the unsaved, who had worshipped Satan or his image, would not live again until a thousand years had passed. Then Satan would be released and would deceive the nations, but it was his destiny to be cast into a lake of fire and brimstone, there to experience eternal torment. Death and hell, and everyone not inscribed in the book of life, were also to be cast into the fiery lake. Then would follow a new and timeless dispensation of heavenly and earthly glory.

Constance Rourke's book touches on the second of these millennial concepts (cited in the preceding paragraph), sometimes confused with the first. Regarding that view—the indefinite period of divine favor—the opening verses of Revelation 21, particularly the fifth verse, actually serve as a refrain in *Trumpets of Jubilee*. The first heaven and earth passed away, and John "saw a new heaven and a new earth," and then a "new Jerusalem," descending from God. Death was to be eliminated, as well as sorrow, crying, and pain. "And he that sat upon the throne said, Behold, I make all things new."

The connection between the idea of an enduring era of glorious peace, prosperity, and truth: the heaven-on-earth or millennial age—and the harsh doctrines of Calvinism and Puritanism, which so strongly influenced early American life and thought—is left vague in Constance Rourke's book. But since *Trumpets of Jubilee* has to do with these seemingly disparate matters, in their relation to the American experience, the link cannot be overlooked or taken for granted. What brought together the "making of all things new" by the religious millenarians and utopian reformers, and the inflexible original-sin theology of powerful Protestant zealots, was—judging from the evidence—popular submission to an authority based on the Bible or on some other spiritual system. Yet what set the two ideologies apart—the principle of compensation—was itself a kind of negative connection.

The millennial and other utopian movements, with their hope of an ideal society for all (followers), served often as antidote to the bleak stringencies of Calvinist theology. The latter's rejectionist view regarding man's chances for eradicating his original sin and subsequent indelible guilt, and for achieving self-improvement, evoked the obvious counterreaction. Man could at will live a satisfying, irreproachable, and self-improving life on earth, simply by following the precepts of a particular communal sect. Woman too, for once, might even be offered a position of parity with man. And by attempting to "make all things new," these movements could retain the spirit of the Christian Bible while correcting an outmoded interpretation of that Bible: i.e., the Calvinist interpretation, with its T.U.L.I.P. doctrines stressing man's prior guilt and his essential helplessness regarding his own salvation. Or, a non-Bible-inspired approach, such as the socio-mathematical one of the Fourier socialists (which *Trumpets of Jubilee* discusses at length), might replace an earlier Christian form.

But these are generalities. To recall again a scanting on the part of Rourke's book, there are the significant details of the career of John Calvin (1509–1564), his interpretations of biblical doctrine (in his *Institutes*, ca.1536), and his influence in the establishment of theocratic governments in Geneva and elsewhere throughout the Western world, including colonial New England. Space does not permit an analysis of his varied philosophical and theological borrowings, or of his restrictive codes: some of them contrary to the spirit of the Protestantism that he himself was helping to shape. Hence, the reader is directed to an informative review of the origins of Calvinism, and its far-reaching effects. Such a useful summary may be found in chapter 21 ("John Calvin") of Will Durant's *The Reformation* (1957). A few comments, however, are necessary here.

An unusually magnetic person of intense fervor and enormous learning, Calvin was the very model of the energetic zealot who develops a new, powerful movement within an existing religion. His favoring of the middle class, their practical virtues, and an expanding economy (matters discussed briefly by Durant), and the authoritative control he was able to exert over vast, credulous populations, made possible a dynamic new order in Western societies. The principle of "election" (according to the *American Heritage Dictionary:* "Predestined salvation, especially as conceived by Calvinists"), though it contradicted the Christian beliefs in salvation through faith and/or good works, held enormous appeal for self-confident and aggressive business entrepreneurs and leaders (or would-be leaders) in other areas of life. In line with this reasoning, only a limited number of Christians were to be redeemed after death, as God saw fit. Period. But—*sotto voce*—surely a worthy individual such as oneself must merit God's special favor? Rourke's treatment of the Beechers, allowing for all of the wrenching vicissitudes they experienced, suggests somehow this continuous fierce, self-confident drive toward a hoped-for if often uncertain victory: a Cross-for-a-Crown victory of the "elect," the saved.

Certain pluses and minuses in Calvinism and its ramifcations ought not to be overlooked. These assets and liabilities have their place—though they are not always italicized—in Rourke's "contrapuntal design" of light and dark, hope and gloom. I touch on them here to indicate that the chiaroscuro effect in *Trumpets of Jubilee* has various interesting and interrelated sources.

The minuses first. An overwhelming authority figure like Calvin does not willingly entertain opposing views or challenges to his (divinely constituted?) authority. Thus it is generally, with incumbent leaders and successful purifiers and reformers of an existing order; they cease their trouble–making. The more dangerous the heresy or other challenge to authority becomes, the more intolerant is likely to be the reaction from the seat of power. This pattern was only too well established by the time of our Revolutionary War, the period during which *Trumpets of Jubilee* begins. The English Puritans, taking a good bit of their inspiration from John Calvin's doctrinal and political break (in his stronghold, Geneva) with the Roman Catholic Church, had broken with their own state church (Anglican), which itself—under Henry VIII—had broken with Rome. And in the resulting bitter factional quarrels of the Puritans, and of their American descendants (Presbyterians, Independents or Congregationalists, and Pilgrims)—some of which quarrels figure prominently in Rourke's chapter on Lyman Beecher—there was a violent rejection of contrary religious views, a sharp divisiveness among Christians, that might be interpreted as an important part of Calvin's legacy.

One historic example: Roger Williams's *The Bloudy Tenent of Persecution* (1644), a defense of his supposedly heretical views against the official position of John Cotton and the Massachusetts General Court.

And now the pluses. As already hinted, there is the enormous impact of Calvinism on the stronger, more self-assertive spirits in—among various domains—the world of commerce. This was felt in the form of the Protestant ethic, that subtle rationale for self-improvement and increasing control of the environment. It is a bit ironic that this progressive thrust—seen in figures as great as Benjamin Franklin and as small as the neighborhood tradesman—derived in part from a religious philosophy of hopeless gloom, guilt, and doom. Yet artful loopholes of reasoning breached the fortifications of the latter, enabling the able-minded to remain adherents of a Calvinist faith (Presbyterianism or Congregationalism, for example), while working out their own itinerary to salvation. This tendency to adapt Calvinism to personal wishes and needs is fascinatingly treated, passim, in Rourke's chapters on the Beecher clan. For another positive feature, in addition to the Protestant ethic, there is the democratizing effect it exerted, through its encouragement of popular education.

Durant, uninhibitedly critical of Calvin and the religious movement he brought into being, has good things to say about that system's stoicism. It "made the strong souls of the Scottish Covenanters, the English and Dutch Puritans, the Pilgrims of New England." This stoicism "encouraged brave and ruthless men," according to Durant, "to win a continent and spread the base of education and self-government until all men could be free." Those choosing "their own pastors soon claimed to choose their governors, and the self-ruled congregation became the self-governed municipality. The myth of divine election justified itself in the making of America." But ironic and suggestive—considering Calvin's persecution of "heretics" (example: the burning of Servetus), and the theological battles (traceable to Calvinistic rigidities) Lyman Beecher was at times embroiled in—is Durant's historical perspective on how the Western world, including America, benefited from the Calvinistic legacy: "the pride of divine election changed into the pride of work and accomplishment."[2]

More will now be said about Rourke's five biographical subjects, in relation to various features of her "contrapuntal design," and to her other purposes in writing *Trumpets of Jubilee.*

II *Despair of Heaven or Hope of Earth*

Underlying Constance Rourke's pattern of organization in *Trumpets of Jubilee*, deeper than the outline of her five entertaining biographical sketches and her "double helix" of light and dark, gloom and hope, is a controlling idea that some close readers of her work must already have observed. That is, her strongly felt need to construct a world of the imagination that would give her a sense of security through continuity with the American past, by means of the binding force of tradition. Her use of the "wilderness" concept—she felt that America of the 1920s, like America of the 1840s and 1850s, had to "make a world out of a wilderness"— suggests her personal attachment to pioneer (maternal) ancestors who had had to do just that. It suggests also her well-known feeling for drama—in the uncomplicated sense of "stage entertainment."

What she did in *Trumpets* was not merely to dramatize five colorful, successful, bigger-than-life figures—though her foreword and to a lesser extent her epilogue make it clear that she was doing this, among other things: "At certain times [i.e., "that middle period of our history"] and in certain places [i.e., "our own country"] popularity becomes a highly dramatic mode of expression."[3] She was actually setting the stage for a drama of the American character, focusing on the middle nineteenth century but really spanning the century. The setting was a kind of wilderness, because in her view a "society," a "social identity," at that time did not yet exist in our nation. And, since she responded deeply to the image and implications of "wilderness," as her books *Davy Crockett* and *Audubon* show, and at the same time was concerned with bringing the past to bear on the present,[4] *Trumpets* poses at least two essential questions. First, what happened to the five pioneering characters—the father and two of his children, and two other dauntless trailblazers? Second, how can the drama of American pioneers in the "wilderness" (so to speak) best be presented, to give it meaning for readers of the later 1920s?

By way of hinting at an answer to the first question since the matter will soon be taken up: despite the book's title, the five "lives" of American success-figures did not, ipso facto, end in success or happiness. There were dramatic crises and ordeals, as others have observed; and a good indication of Rourke's overall assessment of things, based on her deep psychological involvement

in her material, is given in the epilogue. Referring to the classic
revival in earlier American culture, and its suggestion of peace—
but quite possibly thinking of the cultural influences dealt with in
Trumpets (and of what they meant to her five subjects), she had
this to say. The pioneer's moving "toward established modes" was
"part of the irony of his position—when all things were to be made
new!—and part of the promise": the reason being, "the reminis-
cence of a tradition may sometimes enclose a passionate wish, as
well as a passionate sense of failure."[5]

As for the second question—how to present the drama of
American pioneers in the "wilderness"?—a partial answer is,
through the notion of "magnitude." I have touched on these
matters at the beginning of this chapter, but their importance for
Rourke's study must be taken in gradually. She sensed, in the latter
1920s, the importance of size in modern life and in technology, as
well as in man's relation to the entire universe. And, I suspect, she
drew on very early associations with the colossal, as witnessed by
her writing so feelingly of folklore giants like Paul Bunyan and
Davy Crockett ("with sunrise in his pocket"). Thus, summing up
the turbulent nineteenth century of her Beechers, of Greeley and
Barnum, and of a poet of American democracy like Whitman, she
could write: "Magnitude seems the single positive legacy of that
forgotten time." What it held "for that smaller world" was "a hope
and a promise, a token of new eternities, a sense of wonder."
Seeing this quality in her five popular representatives, she felt
almost as if they were transcending ordinary limits; it was as if
"their errands were [really] great errands of the human spirit."[6]

If the projection of the notion of "magnitude," through five
immense personalities, only partially answers the question of how
to present Constance Rourke's "wilderness" production (as I have
termed it), the remainder of the answer—possibly the bulk—is:
through the striking antitheses referred to earlier, the jubilee-
trumpets and Calvinistic repressions, and their light and dark
connotations. These serve as mood-shifts in her drama; they also
have a strong influence on the action. Rourke evoked an atmosphere of dramatic entertainment through her continual spotlight-
ing of one or another of two major cultural forces in nineteenth-
century America, and their effect on the American character (as
seen in a few representative characters): despair of heaven, and
hope of earth.

The "despair of heaven" is the moral climate which masked for many Protestants (with the possible exception of the very self-confident ones) a dubious "hope of heaven": that is, the Calvinist-Puritan belief in erring Everyman's Original and continuing, well-nigh ineradicable, Sin.

Lyman Beecher's story, as Rourke tells it, is heavily shadowed by this awareness of a divine indictment. But he is depicted as so bouncy and energetic a person that with all his disheartenments—among them financial setbacks and administrative crises as head of Cincinnati's Lane Seminary, bereavements, and serious doctrinal conflicts with church officials—one senses that he was not readily disabled by adversity or even by the Calvinist air he breathed. Beecher's native Connecticut, in the last quarter of the eighteenth century, remained staunchly Calvinist. (Jonathan Edwards, the "Great Awakening" Calvinist preacher of eighteenth-century New England, had died in 1758.) But Beecher himself grew up in the farm household of his Uncle Lot, who had moved from Puritanism to Episcopalianism (i.e., the American version of Anglicanism).

Beecher entered Yale College in 1793, when its original Orthodox course—Puritan/Calvinist—had already bent in the direction of Deism, with its idea of the perfectibility of man, and its echoes of the French Revolution and portents of democracy. Thus orthodoxy itself, which underlay Connecticut's government, appeared to be threatened. At stake was its embodiment in the *Standing Order*, which purported to copy the divine scheme: "the orthodox as the elect, its ministry at the seat of power, and the solid rock of Federalism mixed in its foundations." Two years later, with the death of Yale President Ezra Stiles and his replacement by Jonathan Edwards's grandson, Timothy Dwight, Yale regained the character of a church-based school. Beecher responded sympathetically to Dwight, who believed in an enlargement of man's freedom of will (with corresponding accountability), yet described effectively the Calvinist's undeviating position in these terms: "never secure in his hope, always exultant in his worship." The severely Puritanical Dwight told his hearers that righteousness must constantly be sought after, though it was without value in the scheme of things. Each human action, because of Adam's sin, "was evil unless accomplished in a state of grace," and it was up to God's will whether grace would be granted.[7]

Throughout his long life Beecher would labor, preach, suffer, and agonize; the object of all these efforts, and his nemesis, was the near-hopelessness of a Calvinist theological system embodied in Presbyterian, Congregational, or Plan of Union authority. Under the latter arrangement, a fragile partnership annulled during his lifetime, he could preach in either of the two above-named churches. In pulpits at East Hampton, Long Island; Litchfield, Connecticut; Boston; and Cincinnati, where he was also president of the precarious Lane Theological Seminary—he would contend against indifference, certain dangerous new beliefs, evangelical rivals, and attackers within his own church authority.

In Beecher's earlier years, the congregations and church leaders demanded unceasing reassurance from the pulpit that man's unspeakable puniness and natural opposition to God were the essential facts of life. That opposition explained both the universality of sin and the suitability of what God had in store for man. In Litchfield, in the early 1800s when Beecher held a pulpit there, pleasures—to say nothing of very minor vices—were frowned on or forbidden outright. During what Rourke described as a renascence of Puritanism, at this period, even fiddle playing was disapproved of, yet somehow this did not deter Beecher from enjoying his own fiddle on occasion. But temperance was an important popular reform, and Beecher spoke out forthrightly in support of the cause.

One of his critics, at the time he was at the Hanover Church in Boston, was a Dr. Noah Porter of Andover Seminary, who took issue with him on, among other things, the very controversial subject of "means." Porter argued that Beecher depended too heavily on "means". This term, in Rourke's explanation, signifies "the efforts of the anxious soul to attain a saving faith"; it comprises "prayer, repentance, righteous living." If that soul were able to employ "means" to make its own way to salvation, what then "became of the doctrine of election, of instantaneous regeneration, of an illimitable divine sovereignty?" Porter's objection was that Beecher had ceased concerning himself with God's agency (sovereignty, in other words) and was dealing only with the other (unimportant) half of Calvinism: man's agency.

Beecher was involved in much more of this kind of anguished disputation. Regarding the subject of infant damnation, he would have none of it—selective as he was, in the matter of Calvinist theology. "None of it?" his critics carped. "And he dared to say that no other Calvinist, in his experience, believed in it either?" As a result, Calvinists and their natural enemies, the Unitarians, both leaped in and began to assail his argument. "Just when did the allegedly spotless babes put on corruption?" "Wouldn't this (supposed) post-natal depravity conflict with the 'imputation' doctrine?" "What spiritual state were these new-born immaculates in? Not a state of innocence, surely—for what would become of the doctrine of *Adam's Fall*?"

Lyman Beecher's famous heresy trial in 1835 was based on charges brought against him by the Reverend Joshua Wilson, a leader of the Old School faction of the Presbyterian Church. Beecher, he claimed, was guilty of hypocrisy in not always adhering to the Westminster Confession, in scanting official Presbyterian teaching (for example, the "inability" doctrine) and in not having had a bona fide relationship with the Presbyterian Church itself. Arguing in his own behalf, Beecher drew proper distinctions; for example, in regard to "inability": man had the natural ability to fulfill God's commands, but ever since Adam's Fall, man lacked the moral ability to do so. With the force of his arguments and, possibly, his personality, Beecher was acquitted of the charges; he won a second time, when the prosecutor's appeal was rejected.

No lasting triumph for Beecher, however. The Old School synods in the Presbyterian Church, bent on stifling Congregationalist influence as well as heretical views in their preachers—and unhappy with certain of Beecher's views—expelled the New School synods. This meant that Beecher, owing to his identification with the latter, was "cut off from the faith of his origins, cast first into one diminished church and then into another, and identified with a cause," slavery, which meant little to him. This slavery issue had recently wiped out Lane Seminary's student body; the students had been proabolition, the trustees had repressed their abolitionist endeavors, and Beecher had been staunchly neutral on the subject.

One of Beecher's daughters, Harriet, married the theologian and philologist Calvin Stowe, who outdid his father-in-law in the matter of orthodoxy. Another daughter, Catherine, was an ardent antifeminist at a time when the whole philosophy of women's rights was still in its early stages of formulation. She felt a call to proclaim "woman's acceptance of her inferior place"; this reflected "the Puritan mode, which" on occasion was applied practically, as her father's example showed. As for Beecher's sons: through his influence and precedent, all seven entered the Protestant ministry. But the patriarch himself, after a lifetime of contending and struggling, and with his end perilously near (it was 1863, and the country was torn by a Civil War), was racked by anxiety. His theological uncertainties became horrifying stabs of doubt. Was he really of the elect? Would he be saved, after all? How would he face the actual process of dying? But then his essential self-confidence returned, and the old, resilient Lyman Beecher rallied once again: his spirit was proof against those harrowing doubts. To judge from his self-contented response at the very end, he was indeed one of the chosen.[8]

On a certain occasion during her childhood, Harriet Beecher, the seventh of Lyman Beecher's nine children by his first wife (four more were born to his second), believing herself to be saved, resisted her father's strict application of the principle of election. "Marshaling the reasoned elements of the Calvinist faith," Beecher quickly showed her where she had erred. Thus her emotions were put under a severe strain. Resentment at his charging *her* with Original Sin gave way to gaiety, and when she was rebuked for this, she fell into a state of listlessness studded with periods of unhappiness, but withal she wanted others to love her.[9]

The dramatic tensions of Calvinistic gloom and buoyant human spirits, employed by Constance Rourke to represent Lyman Beecher's colorful history, are replicated but with somewhat different overtones when Harriet Beecher is brought onstage. She is a heroine who is seen to have struggled and suffered in a more poignant way than did her father; hence there is a stronger basis for reader identification. Rourke places a great deal of emphasis on the oppression and repression Harriet was to endure at the hands of men. Specifically, they were men who—with their fearful avenging God, with their mandate from the Bible and such authorities as John Calvin, and with their sanction from the American legal and political system—saw to it that women remained in a servile position, domestically centered. *Trumpets*, incidentally, reminds us that Calvinism and the Federalism of the late eighteenth century had certain affinities; and, there may have been other political ramifications of Calvinism in the following century, possibly relating to the perpetuation of slavery.

If, earlier, Harriet's father had set the basic pattern, her husband Calvin enlarged and intensified it. This widower she had cast her lot with was nine years older than herself and deeply committed to the rationale of Calvinism. But he lacked the dynamism that the faith's spokesmen and leaders required. An unstable melancholiac, Stowe was inclined to weep on occasion, suffered from disturbing visions and imaginings—possibly because of some chronic nervous disorder—and showed himself quite unable to take care of his large and growing family. Harriet might break with the Calvinism of her father, might find her husband's helplessness hard to bear, and might even be susceptible to the romantic aura of the novelist Madame de Staël, with whom she firmly sympathized. But there was no way for her to get out from under—unless, possibly, through the escape route of a made-up story about an oppressed Negro slave whose death sets him free at last.

In her brilliant commentary on Mrs. Stowe's *Uncle Tom's Cabin* (1852)—perhaps the best part of *Trumpets*, and justly praised by Hyman in *The Armed Vision*—Constance Rourke, who herself responded so strongly to the novel, was clear on this point. Uncle Tom the martyr was the character with whom Mrs. Stowe identified most closely. She extended the man "a pity akin to self-pity," and provided "him with a mild faith" that she herself had been striving for over the years. The book's themes—"escape, bondage, and rebellion"—served "a public whose heritage" generally was the same as the author's: a public "bred largely in the same faith," but bravely leaving it. *Uncle Tom's Cabin* possessed something that apparently reflected a basic element in the mood of the age.[10]

Constance Rourke's development of Mrs. Stowe's role in this complex nineteenth-century drama is fascinating in the extreme. Drawn from various Beecher family *Lives* and various reference works, as well as from Rourke's highly sensitive impressions of her subject, the character reveals certain interesting contradictions. On the one hand, she opposed her father's morbidly constricting Calvinism; wrote a number of novels in which this straitjacketing system of belief was criticized and disparaged; and suffered from poverty, overwork, and vexing family cares due largely to her emotionally immature husband Calvin, another Calvinist. On the other hand, she herself had been molded by the teachings of

Calvinism: one must be "saved" or face eternal damnation. Yet the transition she was making from the involuntary (unconditional) elect to the voluntary elect seems not to have been very difficult. Moreover, after she had won world-wide fame for her writings and despite her arrogant pretensions to a kind of messianic power in society, she opposed the cause of feminism. Her preference (at least in theory) was for the traditional subservient role for women that her people had always taken for granted. And, whatever her reactions to the stringencies of her father's Calvinistic doctrines, her own religious code held firm.

Thus in 1857, when her son Henry drowned in the Connecticut River, she suffered terrible doubts about his destiny. He had not been converted and she feared for his soul. (Sometime before, when her sister Catherine's fiancé was lost at sea, also in an unconverted state, Lyman Beecher had left no room for hope as far as the young man's fate was concerned.) Championing the cause of Lady Byron, Mrs. Stowe was able to make common cause with her regarding the old faith; Lady Byron seemed to feel that her husband's excesses were due to Calvinism. However, though Mrs. Stowe's spirited defense of her much-maligned noble friend, *Lady Byron Vindicated*, might have led her to extend her advocacy to all women or at least all American women, she drew the line and, assuming the editorship of a domestic journal, confined her further efforts within modest limits.

Deep resentment against men per se, she did feel; still, the thought of Byron's life made her particularly furious. And what she said about Byron and his literary associations matched what her father had said when she was a child, yet her attack on Byron's immorality was more severe. "One of the most rebellious of [Lyman Beecher's] children had given new life to the Puritan tradition" half a century following his journeyings up and down Connecticut in an attempt "to establish an antique censorship."[11]

Henry Ward Beecher had, somewhat like his sister Harriet, consulted creeds quite foreign to Calvinism. After her son Henry's drowning, she had looked into spiritualism. And Henry Beecher, an indifferent student in his school days, was to be a lifelong believer in the dogmas of that brain-bump faith, phrenology. (This pseudoscience ran counter to the ancestral religion, according to Rourke, for this simple reason: the former endowed man with grand "virtues like Firmness, Benevolence, Philoprogenitiveness, and Moral Courage, when" obviously he possessed "no native virtues at all.")

There is more to the matter than this, of course. From Rourke's early discussion of Henry Ward Beecher onward, *Trumpets* indicates a marked diminution of the old-time Calvinism, as its two derivatives from Puritanism—Congregationalism and Presbyterianism—accommodated themselves to the changing times. But while Harriet's brother Henry was affected far less than she, by tensions between Calvinistic gloom (what I have called despair of heaven) and fresh vital spirits (prompting what I have called hope of earth), Rourke's account will continue to keep the reader aware of the former influence, no matter how attenuated it became.

Henry's bride had come from a background similar to his, and yet one important environmental element was lacking: the "lively humor" supplied by Henry's father, which had tempered the severity of their Puritan household. Upon Henry's graduation from Lane Seminary in Cincinnati (of which his father was president), he began his ministerial career in a small Presbyterian church in the village of Lawrenceburg, Indiana—where the tradition of Puritanism was weak and infirm. There he was in harmony with his physical and social environment, but somewhat out of harmony psychologically and spiritually. This foreshadowed the inconsistencies—appearing in *Trumpets* as a series of comic touches superimposed on the book's underlying pattern of dramatic contrasts—that make his ministerial career difficult to take seriously. Henry would represent with striking effectiveness (for a good portion of his life) the allegorical figure of Have It Both Ways.

Called to a church in Indianapolis, he found himself now and then in the grip of religious doubts and spells of laziness. Yet he assailed his audience (at least the male portion) with a series of *Lectures to Young Men.* These sermons in the tradition of Yale's President Timothy Dwight, one of the chief figures in New England's rebirth of Puritanism and a former mentor of Lyman Beecher—whose "'morals campaign'" during Henry's childhood had been part of that tradition. In Henry's *Lectures* one found comparable Puritanical philippics "against idleness, against pleasure, against the arts, the same insistence upon the value of property."[12]

Just at the time when Henry was preparing for ordination, his father—keenly conservative, upholder of Old School doctrines—abruptly embraced the "modern" position. Henry, who had also been espousing the Old School view, at once followed suit.[13]

Thanks partly to Henry's influence, "a solid social censorship was being established," while at the same time Henry in an about-face attacked "social tyranny" (however manifested), though his *Lectures*, in promoting the first effect, precluded the second.

An unusually forceful revivalist and church leader, he was called in 1847 to Brooklyn's Plymouth Church. Organized on the Congregational plan, the church was open to him because ministers of his persuasion could work within both the Presbyterian and the Congregational bodies. In his new pulpit Henry was to gain enormous influence as a popular religious leader, and prodigious financial benefits from his grateful, well-heeled congregants. For example, after a solo "grand tour" he made in 1850, Henry began to collect art objects, books, and other expensive items. Responding strongly to the atmosphere of wealth and splendor, he bent his efforts to obtain every token "of that dangerous luxury which only a few years before he had denounced."[14]

The thunderous, flamboyant preaching for which Henry was famous derived from the fiercely predestinarian theology of John Calvin, but its present direction was a vulgar, self-indulgent freedom. Henry gave himself over to the pleasures of the senses, to the many faces of art, to indolence—which he made into a kind of obligation. Once he had pleaded the cause of liberty, the kind that had nothing to do with slavery; now he cried out for "warm and immediate" love. This state of being in love with love itself enveloped his earlier supreme allegiance to God. His theology had taken a pantheistic turn; now he rejected the Calvinistic picture of God: such an aloof deity presiding over reprobation (for the many) and election (for the few) froze him to the bone. Henry could now declare his congregants gods, thus doing even greater violence to his father's religion.

A superb pulpit actor, Henry effectively dramatized for his huge audiences his moods and convictions of the moment. He made of his church service a spectacle, an entertainment. There was, for example, a mock slave auction, which yielded a huge bounty in free-will contributions from his deeply moved congregation. On another occasion Henry even staged a little "John Brown and his chains" number. The crowd "ate that one up" as well. Bursting with energy, he began to involve himself in politics and public affairs; he edited an influential newspaper, the *Independent;* and he wrote a novel entitled *Norwood.*[15]

Henry's adultery charge and the resulting imbroglio (he was in his late fifties when the scandal started) involved: (1) a complicated rivalry with Theodore Tilton, his somewhat irresponsible protégé on the editorial staff of the *Independent;* (2) a tangled relationship with the feminist movement, one of whose leaders was a self-assertive woman named Victoria Woodhull; and (3) a series of other unwise entanglements, particularly one with Tilton's wife. The charges and countercharges, lawsuits, political overtones, etc. are too involved to be summarized here. No court of inquiry was ever to find Henry guilty of adultery with Mrs. Tilton. The original accusations, brought by Victoria Woodhull and Theodore Tilton, must be weighed against their unconventional views and aberrant behavior. Considering the space Rourke allots to the whole matter of Henry's supposed relationship with Elizabeth Tilton, she is too vague about his actual dealings with her. From the account in *Trumpets* the reader may get the impression that Henry and the lady had never been in contact at all, and that Henry was victimized by a completely baseless charge of adultery. But there were numerous ironies in this long-drawn-out Beecher "affair" and its ramifications; at least one concerned Puritanism.

Victoria Woodhull, not long before her newspaper letter in 1872 hinting at the liaison between Henry Beecher and Elizabeth Tilton, had been preaching the need for the elimination "of legal constraint": that is, freedom to live one's life as one wished. In *Woodhull and Claflin's Weekly* (a newspaper she edited with her sister) and in at least one large public meeting, this inconsistent advocate of certain eccentric movements including spiritualism cried out for "'Untrammeled Lives!'" Unconvincingly, Constance Rourke exculpates this demand "from gross implications," stating that Mrs. Woodhull "denounced the Puritan tradition as maintained by both church and state."

At about this time, Mrs. Woodhull's newspaper writings on the marriage question—she wished to lead a social revolution to alter the institution of marriage—and on Henry Beecher's doings were discovered by a self-made commissar of vice suppression, Anthony Comstock. He had her printing facilities demolished, persecuted her, and successfully prosecuted her. Then, as head of the Society for the Suppression of Vice, Comstock began a closer inquiry, based on a spy system, into the background of offenders against public morals. His endeavors to prevent a public showing of Hiram Powers's nude statue, *The Greek Slave*, led to a heated "discussion of the relation of Puritanism to art." Opponents found a similarity in Comstock's S.S.V. and those New England "Moral Societies which had been established" half a century earlier "as a final thrust for authority [by] the older Puritans."[16]

As for Henry Ward Beecher himself: by the late 1870s and early 1880s (he would live until 1887) he had become fairly secularized, accommodating himself to Darwin's *The Descent of Man* (1859), accepting progress, finding religion and science in harmony with each other. He even left the Congregational Association, to an extent fraternizing with nonbelievers, and showing a friendly disposition toward "the great agnostic," Bob Ingersoll.[17]

It is interesting that *Trumpets of Jubilee* appeared in the same year (1927) as Sinclair Lewis's study of an unprincipled and roguish revivalist preacher, *Elmer Gantry*. Reactions to Lewis's novel were wildly mixed. One writer, Paxton Hibben, objecting to another's declaration that such a man as Elmer Gantry never existed, "devoted his review in the *New Masses* to a list of known debaucheries by clergymen whom he named, the first of them being Henry Ward Beecher."[18]

Constance Rourke's treatment of the lively and enterprising Horace Greeley, two years older than Henry Ward Beecher, shows an even greater, if less dramatic, dissipation of the glooms of Calvinism-Puritanism than was the case with the latter. The mood of light and hope and jubilee, in *Trumpets*, will intensify so that the progressive element in the American character can be projected more forcefully.

Greeley would make his name as the founder and editor of the *New York Tribune*, as the "Go West, young man" pragmatist who had a town in northern Colorado named for him, and to a lesser extent as the unsuccessful Liberal–Republican candidate for president in 1872. He was born in southern New Hampshire, in a region whose inhabitants did not come under the influence of Puritanism. Their reputedly dubious morals aroused the criticism of Yale's Timothy Dwight, "tireless promoter of the Puritan renascence," who was of the opinion that the people's decline in morals brought about "worldly failure." In his teens Greeley was bound as an apprentice by his chronically unsuccessful father to the owners of a newspaper in the western Vermont village of East Poultney. Perhaps because the dreary labor there demanded psychological relief, or possibly for the reason that the older folks in this part of New England were still under Puritan influence, he was ready for a particular kind of nontraditional religious faith. He, apparently like other young folk thereabouts, found this in Universalism, a cheerful theology completely rejecting Calvinism, and declaring that man's destiny involved continual progress and, finally, universal human happiness.

It may well be that something of Universalism's dynamic optimism affected Greeley in the course of his long editorial and political career, during which he espoused such causes as "coöperative labor leagues," the abolition of capital and corporal punishment, the protective tariff, free land, and the Free Soil and antislavery movements. However, by the time of his disastrously futile presidential campaign against Grant in 1872, his old beliefs, according to Rourke, had yielded to time and circumstance. His party's platform was practically devoid of propositions; all that he had left were "his prejudices against liquor, tobacco, and gambling, the outline of a Puritan mode," combined with a vague pacifism. Utterly lost in time, with his vestigial (and perhaps unsuspected) Puritanism, Greeley made a very pathetic figure.[19]

Rourke's concluding dramatic sketch, that of P. T. Barnum, makes particularly interesting reading. Where she obtained all of her materials is unclear; easygoing about reference sources (although her two-page bibliographical note mentions works consulted), she listed only the files of Barnum's ephemeral newspaper, the *Herald of Freedom*, as background. Nevertheless, here at last Rourke's drama of the struggle of our deeply rooted Calvinism-Puritanism against dissent, reform, and indifference will take a sharper turn. That socioreligious system will come under direct attack. In its final response to this challenge it will not give way utterly in the face of stronger group force, but will rather yield outwardly while gaining a certain internal, or psychological, advantage. The mood of this chapter is light and jubilant enough (extending the pattern of the Horace Greeley chapter much further), but the glooms of Calvin's legacy in America will prove themselves stubbornly resistant and potent enough to assume strangely deceptive forms.

Barnum's Connecticut, where he was born in a village called Bethel in 1810, had long been a noisy battleground of orthodox and heterodox religious forces, "in the struggle to entrench Calvinism as a state established religion" and to permit only properly certified adherents to vote. However, the state's tiny settlements, frequently described as clutched "remorselessly in the Puritan grip," embraced a diversified range of political and religious viewpoints, including unbelief, and a variety of social backgrounds. Many people fell into what might be called the lower orders: small tradesmen, innkeepers, peddlers, town drunks and bums, etc. These folk in particular chafed against the religious blue laws, which were designed to keep the Sabbath holy and to suppress intemperance and sexual misconduct. In fact the common people relished playing tricks and jokes on outlanders or on each other, "putting something over" on anyone who was vulnerable, for business or pleasure or simple diversion.

According to Rourke, these Connecticut villagers, beneath "the awful shadow of the Calvinistic doom," managed to live "by their wits" as they found delight in "their natural talents" at the same time carrying out "private anti–Puritan campaigns." Barnum's grandfather, who had been a justice of the peace, could joke it up with the best or worst in the village, and made great sport of violating the blue laws. Neither Barnum's father nor his mother came from an orthodox family, and as a youngster Barnum, whose improvident father had died early, passed his time in the small family inn: "already in public life, a predestined anti-Puritan and a born adventurer."

Around 1831, Barnum—who had by now been a sharp–trading country storekeeper and a lottery entrepreneur—began publishing the *Herald of Freedom*, which attacked not only the ministers and the institution of Calvinism, but "the entire Standing Order." This was done "in the name of Freedom," with Barnum maintaining "that a conspiracy was afoot to restore the old alliance of church and state in Connecticut," although the Puritans' efforts to retain their governmental power center there had ended long before. In the cause of freedom Barnum tried to advance the religious movement of Universalism, that two-decades-old "thorn in the Puritan side." Opposing religious hypocrisy and comparable types of humbug, Barnum let himself in for several libel suits and saw himself oppressed by the same kind of spirit that had emanated from John Calvin.

Considering Barnum's later triumphs as a showman-impresario, there were defeats aplenty for him in the earlier 1830s, owing considerably to Puritan influence: a jail term for libel, failure of his newspaper and of his store, prohibition of lotteries (in 1834), restoration of the blue laws. The Standing Order might have been revoked, but the social norm of "the Puritan mode of conduct" gained in importance. "Respectability and Puritanism" overlapped now to an even greater extent than they had before.

Building on his native propensities for appealing to the crowd through fast talk and exhibitionistic devices, the future circus magnate would before very long begin bringing shows and performers before the public. Early on, he tried unsuccessfully to sign up as a lecturer the writer and lobbyist Anne Royall, whose deep-seated opposition to Calvinism beautifully suited Barnum's ongoing dedication to "the anti-Puritan rebellion"; his attempts to tour Connecticut with a couple of sideshow performers were frustrated, because of the blue laws. Somewhat later, conducting a very small circus through the deep South, he was hampered by Puritanical prejudices against such frivolity, and also by the frivolity and hell-raising of some of the country roughnecks that turned out for his presentations.

Barnum's later relations with the Puritan tradition, which would show its tenacity (through its adaptability) in so many odd ways, make for fascinating reading. He was eventually to put on moral dramas—Bible and temperance shows—by means of fireworks displays and dramatized scenes. Here one finds a touch of classic American humor: the hoax, the deadpan put-on, the burlesque, the travesty. Now the forbidden, morally unacceptable theater (from the Puritanical point of view), thanks to Barnum, was actually offering the Bible and a code of morality to a congregation of sinners. Moreover, as proprietor of his Museum, Barnum mockingly assumed the role of pastor, treating his audience as though it had come to worship in church, while he made any number of jokes at the expense of the Christian ministry. Opposing Puritanism as he did, he nevertheless (in these little pseudodramas) underscored the lesson-teaching element in that way of life. In fact, he might have been a Puritan, for all of his downgrading of the arts and his holding them up to ridicule. After the Civil War, in his last decades as a master showman, Barnum was a strong advocate of temperance as well as of abstinence from tobacco. And wonder of wonders, Barnum actually "advertised the Puritan program."[20]

So much for the dark, Calvinistic strain in Rourke's extended drama of the American social "wilderness" of the early nineteenth century. Her five popular giants had, she felt, to make a world out of this "wilderness": to somehow develop for our scattered and diverse population a social identity with a central tradition and character. This would be done to sustain future generations and provide a framework for their continued growth. As mentioned earlier, just as the stringencies of a slowly waning orthodoxy helped shape that new world (as Rourke conceived it), so too did the opposing force of renovation and jubilation. Sometimes, as in the case of Lyman Beecher, the latter force might actually work in conjunction with the former. The major thrust of this jubilant renewal, however, involved a definite break with traditional belief and life-style—which would have been unthinkable for Lyman Beecher.

Thus, Rourke's most impressive pictures of the effects of the spirit of light and hope, a fitting dramatic contrast to the spirit of the Calvinist legacy, are given in the chapters on Lyman Beecher (paradoxical as it may seem) and Horace Greeley. As for her three other biographical subjects, their association with the "jubilee trumpets" idea seems to be this. Harriet Beecher Stowe fought bravely against tyranny, demanding freedom for oppressed blacks and women. She identified in fact with the character of the Negro slave Uncle Tom and with Lady Byron, whom she tried to redeem from social obloquy in *Lady Byron Vindicated*. Henry Ward Beecher transformed the rigorous Puritanism that had been handed down to him, into a gospel of self-pampering hedonism. P. T. Barnum—like the others, voluble if not overly bombastic, a "bigger-than-life" personality, and a huge popular success—carried his flamboyant theater, his Greatest Show on Earth, throughout the land and to England and Europe as well. He could even maintain a stationary Museum in New York City, for the purpose of bringing entertainment to the masses. Describing the music offered by his traveling spectacle, Rourke mentions brass bands, bell chimes, calliope, steam organ, Scots bagpipers, and a troupe of Negro jubilee singers. But it remains now to look briefly at the material on light, hope, and jubilation (the book's dramatic countertheme) to be found primarily in the chapters on Lyman Beecher and Horace Greeley.

Lyman Breecher, in Rourke's portrait, caught the incipient vibrations of the age, with his Revelation-based hopes for renewal of the human spirit and of his brand of Calvinism. In fact, he seemed to sense an imminent profound renovation of the existing order, a making of all things new, through jubilant rededication to duty. The westward migrations and expansion of our national borders, the limitless possibilities for growth, were somehow reflected in Beecher's new vision of what lay ahead. "The thousand years of predicted happiness was at hand, hastened by the power and the example of the new nation." And Rourke quotes Beecher (apparently from his *Autobiography and Correspondence*, edited by Charles Beecher) to the effect that our country would, through its explosive achievements, revolutionize and free the rest of the world. At that time the jubilee trumpet would be heard and the earth's liberated masses would exalt with hosannas the Son of David.[21]

Among the fierce theological battles over minutiae of doctrine that Lyman Beecher was drawn into by opponents within his own church organization, one was particularly interesting. The charge: he had supposedly taught that man could follow God's commands and, so to speak, perfect himself. If Beecher had actually done so, what would then happen to the precept of man's original and essential corruption, and to other elements of Calvinism (predestination, for example)? Through clever logic-chopping Beecher refuted the accusation that he had thus advocated perfectionism: a doctrine that actually reflected the spirit of the times more than his own reconstructed Calvinism.

The powerful revivalist Charles Finney had been supporting this heretical view of man, which in fact derived from another Christian preacher, John Humphrey Noyes—according to whom, "the Millennium had already begun" and "perfection was now attainable" (accordingly, Noyes had founded a colony of millenarians in Vermont). And, this philosophy of human perfection through the medium of Christ (which seems, though Rourke does not mention it, to hark back to Paul's Epistles) was only one fraction of an increasingly important movement that would help shape American thought through much of the century. That is, a transforming, light- and hope-bringing utopianism. Rourke's survey of religious and secular utopian movements, in the chapter on Lyman Beecher, gives it a special piquancy, but she continues the survey in her chapter on Henry Ward Beecher, and I will include a few notes from that source as well. A host of reformers, self-appointed torchbearers in the conflict-ridden drama presented in *Trumpets of Jubilee*, would—whether they realized it or not—do a great deal to rout the dark, persistently lingering forces of Calvinism.

There was, for example, Jemima Wilkinson with her New Jerusalem colony in the New York wilderness. One particular body of pilgrims left Vermont to look for the Promised Land, but was never heard from again. Joseph Smith and his followers left New York for Ohio and points west, in expectation of Jesus's Second Coming; they carried with them golden tablets, "records of the Lost Tribes, and a buried history which described the new country as chosen for a transcendent destiny from the time of the Flood." There were, among these newly created colonies, "the Shakers, the Harmonists, the Separatists of Zoar, the schismatic Rappites"; the great English industrialist and social reformer Robert Owen anticipated "a new social and political era" which would originate before long in the west. Two of his colonies had been abandoned—New Harmony and Yellow Springs—but a number of other colonies, based on his optimistic and perfectibilitarian view of human nature, were attempting to survive. Other annunciators of change in the existing order appeared on the scene: Victoria Woodhull, who stated that earthlings, alone among all other planetary inhabitants, would uncover the mystery of the universe; Ann Gilchrist; William Miller; John H. Noyes, founder of the utopian colony in Vermont and the Oneida Community in New York.[22]

In the chapter on Horace Greeley, the mood of optimism and jubilation—deriving largely from Rourke's treatment of utopian settlements—contrasts with the man's tribulations (some of which were touched on earlier), particularly at the end of his life. Attacked by North and South for his stand on the Civil War and his attitude toward Negroes, then crushingly defeated in his 1872 presidential bid against Grant—whom he had endorsed in 1868, and finally losing control of his *New York Tribune* (shares in which he had been selling off for years), Greeley made a sad spectacle indeed. And yet Greeley's America was full of promise, or at least gave intimations of better things to come, not only because of the waning of the glooms of Calvinism and Puritanism, but more importantly because people's imaginations were being stirred by new and far-reaching possibilities. The light being shone into darker corners of traditional, nineteenth-century America was a strange, multicolored light.

Around the beginning of the fifth decade, Rourke observes, when Greeley was barely thirty, all sorts of abolishment panaceas were being proposed: the elimination "of money, of rent, of idleness, of meat as a food, of animal labor"; the countless new systems and beliefs portended "an instant Millennium" and "the thousand years of peace seemed to have begun." She describes the Boston convention of 1840, sponsored by a group called "Friends of Universal Progress," where promoters of all sorts of movements got together in a mutual-admiration society: "Abolitionists saluted Agrarians; Grahamites joined with Millerites; Calvinists met on friendly terms with dubious Unitarians," both of which factions mingled "with Vegetarians, Groaners, Come-Outers, Dunkers, and Muggletonians."[23] Parenthetically: hope and fond fancy spring eternal—around three decades later Victoria Woodhull's Universology program, Rourke comments in her chapter on Henry Ward Beecher, claimed to provide the all-inclusive formulaic basis for "the universal reconciliation of all differences and the reign of peace, love, and truth."[24]

One of the major features of the very long, interesting, and powerfully written chapter on Greeley has to do with his involvement in a particular utopian system: the ultrasocialistic program of Fourierism, which was designed to eliminate human competition and replace the traditional family-oriented society with a series of mathematically scaled communal groupings. Through division of labor and personality types, and with due provision for individual emotional outlets, the founder, Charles Fourier (1772—1837), meant to promote universal harmony, social unity, and an all-embracing order of existence.

Greeley came to Fourierism through the founder's energetic disciple in the United States, Albert Brisbane. The idea of togetherness—association, as it was called—especially appealed to Greeley, as did Fourier's doctrine of social rather than political reform of the whole economic system. Greeley must also have responded to another vital element in Fourier's dream wish of social perfection: harmony. Greeley contributed generously to the North American Phalanx colony in New Jersey and became treasurer of another Fourier group, the Sylvania Association of Pennsylvania; he would also pay visits to George Ripley's Brook Farm near Boston, which had attempted to emulate the Fourier pattern, as well as the Universalist colony in Hopedale, which apparently did not follow Fourier.

But Greeley's having committed himself to the principle of association ᶳᴹa la Fourier would prove to be one more of his strategically ill-advised moves. The widespread Fourier movement fell apart, around 1846—for a variety of reasons. Its implicit sexual-freedom policy aroused public indignation, particularly after Greeley debated Fourier's philosophy with Henry J. Raymond, a former writer for Greeley's *Tribune*. Severe critics of Fourier's scheme attacked not only its provocative element of association, but the idea that social evils could be eliminated. They held that human nature itself, the root of those evils, was incapable of being changed for the better. Here then, in what might have been a cheerful and brightly lit chamber of American experience, the heavy, dismal, leftover furniture of the Calvinist philosophy of man would still cast its dispiriting shadow. Additionally, the Fourier communards tended to be agriculturally and financially inept. Diminishing faith in the system itself helped ensure that their impracticality would not be compensated for, by the power of muscle and determined spirit.

Thus, more sour notes in the jubilee-trumpet fanfare of the 1800s. Embarrassed, in the face of mounting criticism, by his involvement with the association concept, Greeley would cease writing about it in the *Tribune*. However, he continued as one of the directors of the North American Phalanx and retained his affiliation with the American Union of Associationists, becoming president of that body in 1849. Perhaps because he often worked against his own best interests, Greeley's other attempts to apply the principle of association—as in his joint-stock scheme to share *Tribune* ownership with senior staffers, and in his involvement with labor-league cooperatives—were quite unsuccessful. By the end of the 1840s, he had even lost his ties with labor, because of his opposition to trade unions and to the instrument of the strike.

In summary, what Constance Rourke caught from her five characters, I feel, was a world of the imagination which she thought of, first, as a wilderness—such as her pioneer ancestors had braved. An unforgettable sentence of hers in *Trumpets* (on the subject of Fourierism) suggests this idea to me. "*Like a great* pavanne, *or a child's dream of a far* country, or a perpetual circus, the Fourieristic scheme spread its sweetly assembled elements."[25] The Beechers, Greeley, and Barnum—all coming from small eastern villages or farms—through their distinctive talents, energy, and force of personality: their magnitude—created for themselves an abode of the spirit which would replace their pastoral origins. They transformed or banished altogether the dark, wild forces of Calvinism—partaking to an extent of the pervasive, intoxicating fumes of millennial utopian hope—and they helped bring about freedom at last for Negroes, women, and the chronically enshackled self. These five possessed an indefinable quality which would make them giants of popular legend. As such, Constance Rourke apparently felt, they would be unusually impressive and entertaining to ordinary Americans. They might also point the way—to readers of the wild discordant 1920s—back to a challenging but somehow more comfortable America of the mid-1800s, where people of any size or stature could still feel a sense of kinship and a continuity of tradition.

CHAPTER 4

Girls of the Golden West

*T*ROUPERS *of the Gold Coast or the rise of Lotta Crabtree* appeared in 1928, a year after *Trumpets of Jubilee*, and would seem to be a kind of interlude between Constance Rourke's far more significant performances in *Trumpets* and *American Humor*. In fact, it reads almost like a dream book or wish book: Rourke's private fantasy of romance. As with her strange, negligible envoi to the Horace Greeley chapter in *Trumpets*, her biographies of Davy Crockett and Audubon, and the opening passage of *American Humor*, it is written in a quasi-fictional style. But it sadly lacks narrative quality, so lifeless are the real-life characters and so cluttered is it with theatrical and topographical minutiae. Ironically, though it appears devoid of literary merit, it is possible that this modest trifle of a book, more than any other book Rourke wrote in her lifetime, represents the inmost leaf of her being. First I shall briefly discuss the relation between the lives of subject and author; following that, I shall say something about how *Troupers* fits into the entire body of Constance Rourke's writing.

Troupers is primarily about Lotta Crabtree (1847–1924), a popular American stage entertainer, from childhood onward, in the mining-camp areas of California and Nevada after the Gold Rush created a sizable new audience for actresses, actors, and all manner of theatrical performers, in what was to become the so-called Golden West. Lotta's stage career extended also to New York, Boston, and many other cities and towns across the continental United States, but the book's aim seems to be to stress the extended area around San Francisco and Sacramento. Lotta, a legendary golden girl in the flesh, peers forth from Rourke's welter of archival details of all the plays, stage entertainments, stellar performers (Lola Montez, Adah Menken, etc.), stage managers, and theater operations, as well as of the geographical descriptions of the rugged terrain that the troupers of the middle 1800s had to cover.

Lotta Crabtree was endowed with many of the qualities and interests (but on a nonintellectual level) that Rourke had, and the two women also shared certain biographical features—as I shall specify shortly. However, Lotta was incredibly successful with the public; roughly half her life was spent amid the smell of the greasepaint and the roar of the crowd. In addition to this, she became extremely wealthy. Thanks partly to her mother's managerial and investment capabilities, Lotta's estate, on her death, came to almost four million dollars.

Considering Rourke's customary restraint, the book is a moderately lively account of what it must have been like to be this fairy sprite. Again and again one gets the feeling that the author is writing about her ideal self: a career lifetime before the footlights; not only popular, but legendary success—allowing for some occupational setbacks and fallow periods; an immense fortune; long, intimate exposure to the roughest frontier existence in the California and Nevada mining camps, as well as to the elegant theatrical life of San Francisco and cities in other parts of the United States; familiarity with the broad middle range of show business experience in the second half of the nineteenth century.

All of which is not to say that Constance Rourke secretly craved the sexual and social freedom enjoyed by actresses upon the wicked stage. But could she really have been a frustrated actress, in real life too inhibited or constrained even to indulge in little theater or amateur theatricals? Whether or no, there seems to have been very much in Lotta's life and career that Rourke admired. Why else would she have spent so much time researching and writing about a stage star of the last century, who for all her contemporary fame, does not seem by any stretch of the imagination to have warranted a full-length biography? Whatever Lotta shared with Constance Rourke, does make for a special kind of story, however, which will throw some light on the why and how of this particular treatment of the actress's life.

Each was closely attached to her mother, who to a great extent ran the other's professional and personal life, in the absence of a man. Constance Rourke's father had died when she was very young; Lotta's ever-wandering father, though he rejoined her mother from time to time over the years until he died (two sons

were born of these infrequent contacts), was never with Lotta
long enough or effectively enough to have had a paternal influence on her. Earlier in this book I alluded to the remarks in Lynn's
introduction to *Trumpets of Jubilee*: the "too-close bond" between
mother and daughter in the case of the Rourkes and the case of the
Crabtrees; and the autobiographical element in *Trumpets*. And I
spoke of the statement, in *Troupers*, that Lotta remained young
while Mrs. Crabtree aged prematurely. This seems, from what I
have observed of photographs of the Rourke ladies, to fit Constance and her mother as well.

Speaking of Lotta's early close contacts with the flashy, sensa-
tional, and inconstant Lola Montez, Rourke mentions the training
benefits Lotta received from her, comments on the oddity of Mrs.
Crabtree's allowing the relationship to exist (later she would hide
her daughter from Lola), and then makes an interesting remark.
"Severely conventional Mrs. Crabtree always was; and all her life
Lotta was to preserve an almost incredible innocence." Sometime
in the middle 1850s Lotta and her mother—who was now
skillfully directing the child's "career" as an entertainer and
actress, were again in San Francisco. Nothing else being available,
Lotta was put to work doing song-and-dance numbers in harbor-
side auction rooms, then in garish saloons frequented by shady
gamblers and ladies of pleasure. Unwilling to expose the child to
these people any longer than was necessary, Mrs. Crabtree took
Lotta off the floor the moment the act ended. Rourke adds: Lotta's
mother "made the final stockade," drawing around her daughter
"that ring of disconcerting fire that was to surround her for many
years, perhaps for the remainder of her life."

The two immediately following remarks about Mrs. Crabtree's
personality are suggestive merely. They may or may not apply to
Constance Rourke's case, although the latter comment is suggestive in light of the next Rourke book, *American Humor*. "Hers was
a strange impulse, that kept the child so closely to herself, yet so
tirelessly before a mixed public. Grimly resolute, she cultivated
humor, because it would pay, perhaps because of some hidden
fund of amusement within herself which seemed destined to find
no other outlet."

By age sixteen, Lotta had become a much more versatile singer,
entertainer, and actress, having played in every manner of theater
and improvised showhouse along the Pacific Coast between San
Francisco and southern Oregon, and inland beyond the Sacra-

mento area as far as Virginia City, Nevada. For all her agreeable,
friendly contacts with all the other stage performers Lotta met
and worked with along the way, in Rourke's interpretation, she
"suffered from the disadvantage of isolation. Except when they
were in the mountains the Crabtrees seldom mingled with the
shifting mob of actors; they hardly seemed theater people at all."
Fittingly, the girl stage artist was called "Miss Lotta the Unapproachable." "That ring of fire which her mother had first drawn
around the child was now widened and burned more fiercely.
Even outside the theater Lotta had few companions." Here Rourke
might have been writing directly of her own experiences.

Then follows a brief anecdote from Lotta's reminiscences in her
old age. A proper young man had wanted to take her riding in his
horse-and-buggy, but Mrs. Crabtree sent him off. Lotta had then
gone outside hoping merely to get another look at the friendly lad.
Considering how cut off Lotta was from close contacts offstage—
partly because her mother saw to it that she was shielded from all
the disreputables in the variety houses and bars where she
performed—and taking into account the strenuous schedule Lotta
was forced to follow, "The odd circumstance was that Lotta
seemed to possess an unflagging momentum of her own."

The mid-1860s found Lotta, under her mother's direction,
performing on the East Coast, in the Middle West, and in the
South: acting in a series of light comedies and melodramas,
singing and dancing—sometimes in blackface, sometimes dressed
as a boy. One little play, kept for a considerable time in her
repertoire—*Nan the Good for Nothing*—held the "kind of part she
was always to favor, that of the ragged little romp who dips into
all sorts of rough comedy business, dances like a street arab, is pert
and rude but engaging, and comes to a good end."

An indication of the extent to which Lotta Crabtree's personality must have intrigued Rourke is given in a particular passage of
Troupers, close to the end. Probing rhetorical questions are raised
about this aloof, repressed, and mother-dominated stage performer, who did not crack under the strain but instead maintained
two different subpersonalities. Rourke's probing here is very
important, not only for what it reveals about her own temperament but also for the way in which it foreshadows her handling of
the subject matter in her next book, *American Humor*.

"Where did it come from," she asks, "that wellspring of lively
fun and mounting airy vivacity? What kept it full and overflow-

ing?" Lotta had continued this way for almost three decades, "with undiminished comic force. In those early tours long ago in the mountains had she caught some deep humor or a wild assurance, a surcharged gayety which was to last for a lifetime? Or had she found an obscure capacity for pleasure deeply caught within herself?" This she had retained despite "a narrowing personal experience" and in the absence of new contacts. Now follows a more pointed observation by Constance Rourke on the development of the comic spirit in an individual. "A sense of humor is sometimes developed in comparative solitude, a sense of fun or broad comedy almost never."

Which makes the author raise this question, and the reader cannot help wondering if it held any personal reference: "Was her temperament simple?" Strangely now, Rourke sums up the supposed personality traits and other characteristics—some superficial, some deeper—that a large number of photographs of Lotta reveal. She is seen as a bewitching, wistful charmer, strong but delicate, gracefully humorous, rebellious enough (at least once) to hold a smoking cigar in her hand. What conclusion does Rourke draw from the broad range of expressions and mannerisms in Lotta's photographs? "Something prisoned was suggested in all that amplitude—wild orbits contained within herself like her passionate temper, with a sweetness and tenderness which could hardly emerge in her boisterous comedy." Was it really? Could Rourke have discerned all this in the pictures? And again she brings up the matter of Lotta's unusually wide, or close, "companionship with her audiences" in contrast with her lack of "personal companionship." Speaking next of the actress's always having "been surrounded by crowds, and also by powerful, intriguing personalities," the author adds: "Within her own compass she too possessed an unmistakable power, which never came to an entire fruition." How could Rourke have known this? Did her informants (listed on p. xii of the salutation)—who had performed with Lotta on the stage or had otherwise been acquainted with her—give the information to the author? And, leading up to the matter of Lotta's stage retirement in 1891, Rourke says something that does not seem *to me* likely to have been said by any of her informants who had known Lotta. "One sees her through years, at first all but overwhelmed as she passed among greater figures, then gradually emerging in her own right, but becoming more and more solitary with all her iridescent charm, as she traveled down the decades."

Only a few interesting hints of comparison between Lotta and Constance Rourke remain. (It should be kept in mind that Lotta had two younger brothers, while Rourke was an only child; however, Mrs. Crabtree's involvement with the boys, judging from the account in *Troupers*, never encroached on her utter absorption with Lotta.) In discussing Lotta's reduced scale of activities after her retirement from the stage, Rourke writes: "Marriage for Lotta was out of the question." Newspaper accounts of her romances could be explained as sensationalist publicity material. Briefly "she had been engaged to a young army officer, who had died; a few other small affairs had claimed her. Spectators of the lives of the Crabtrees" attributed "to her mother her failure to marry." However, her "compact temperament" held "a strain of fickleness, something as light as her changing humor, or at least the capacity to make sudden intense reversals; it is doubtful whether any of these interests occupied her for long."[1] One is reminded, oddly enough, of the two young ladies in Rourke's *Dial* stories of 1921, "The Porch" and "Portrait of a Young Woman."

Nelle Curry's unpublished paper quoted earlier, "The Constance Rourkes" (1951), mentions the author's early "elliptical" style, rendered somewhat more understandable as she matured. "Many, however, felt that she was bafflingly complex, impossible ever to know completely." What relates in a curious way to the remarks about Lotta, in the preceding paragraph, is this statement by Miss Curry. Constance Rourke received "several proposals and broke off one engagement, probably because of her basic individualism, love of freedom of action; also, because of fear of danger to her work from domestic preoccupations. Under the impressive, distinguished exterior, she, like her mother, was liable to sudden, capricious revulsions of feeling."[2]

Could the writing of Lotta's story in *Troupers* have arisen from a youthful fixation in middle life? The self seen as a golden girl of (sexless) romance in the Golden West, remaining proudly aloof from a responsive public and all but a small number of friends, while (for all her alluring capriciousness) giving of herself wholeheartedly only to her fostering mother?

Modest as *Troupers* is in every way, it fulfilled more than one basic concern of Constance Rourke. I have said a good deal about the autobiographical material in the book, while leaving out considerably more that could have been added. But it is worth noting that the relation of *Troupers* to the rest of her work can best be understood if that particular element is seen as an integral part of a tangle of interrelated elements. Two passages in *Troupers* make clear how involved the tangle is. At the conclusion of the book the author sums up Lotta Crabtree's life. From an early age "she had lived . . . close to a thronging and insurgent existence, and had all but mixed with many crowds." At times Lotta had experienced loneliness. "Besides the fundamental relationship in which she had found happiness, she had had endless hours of sheer high amusement on the stage." To a remarkable extent "gayety had been her portion." At the beginning of the book, in the salutation, Rourke indicates that *Troupers* resulted from "a mingling of many enthusiasms." Foremost among them was the past, specifically, the time of the Gold Rush—that is, from the end of the 1840s on into the 1860s and beyond: for the most part, in the California-Nevada region. People who lived during the period of this "ardent movement," according to Rourke, "were stirred as few others have been to put into words the novelty and force of their experience. Seldom has a compact era had so ample a personal literature."[3]

Here then are Rourke's personal, preferential, and professional concerns, all intricately interwoven. First, her desire for a sense of community (Lynn in his introduction to *Trumpets* remarks that "thronging" was a favorite word of hers)—for identification with a coherent group whose traditions and needs she might share. Such a group would necessarily be an integral part of the American scene and would add its own lines to the delineation of the American character: Rourke's lifelong concern as a writer. To counterbalance this psychological (if not physical) gregariousness, there was her sense of being cut off from others—the unpleasant feeling, very subtly hinted in various of her works, that there was no effective way to lose herself in a functional community. The story of Lotta Crabtree, so colorless and flat in Rourke's version, must I imagine have projected itself vividly and resonantly in her mind, but in a way that she was simply unable to communicate. Most telling, and requiring no real amplification, is the comment about the fundamental relationship in which Lotta had found happiness. This, from the account in *Troupers*, could refer only to her ties with her mother.

Apropos of the last points, Rourke's biographical subjects were not always chosen from solitary, intensely private individuals. The five in *Trumpets of Jubilee* were largely outgoing types; on the other hand, John James Audubon, Davy Crockett, and the painter Charles Sheeler seem to have been geniune introverts (Crockett, a sometime representative in Congress, less consistently than the other two). Regarding an unusually close relationship between mother and daughter, only the Lotta Crabtree book to my knowledge reflects this quintessential feature of Constance Rourke's own life.

The observation about Lotta's hours of amusement on the stage, and her gayety, reveals once again where Constance Rourke's heart lay and what her temperament was like, despite her close attachment to her mother. Her article on vaudeville (discussed earlier) and her long essay on "The Rise of Theatricals" in the essay collection *The Roots of American Culture* are among her various tributes—*Troupers* being the most prominent—to the life of the theater, in which she took such delight.

It was strange enough, however, for Rourke to praise so lavishly the "personal literature" of those who lived during the Gold-Rush period (extremely obscure works on west coast lore, mentioned in her salutation), when its force was not reflected in her biography. For whatever reason, Rourke was intrigued by mysteries and unsubstantiated claims surrounding the birth or marriage of a particular figure she might be writing about. As she would speculate later about Audubon's controversial origins, she discusses (near the end of the book) various theories about who Lotta's father really was, and about the possibilities of Lotta herself having married and borne a child. But these do not heighten the action of the story or enhance its literary quality in any way. More significantly, though, *Troupers*—in the light of Rourke's remarks about what she called the "ardent movement" (i.e., the Gold Rush) and in the light of her interests in the theater, in a sense of community and tradition, and in regional American life—seems to reflect another essential Rourkean concern. That is, the desirability of creating "a world [of theatrical glamour] out of a wilderness" from the nineteenth-century past for her contemporaries in the late 1920s.

CHAPTER 5

American Humor:
From Smiles to Laughter

I   *A Householder of Mirth*

CONSTANCE Rourke's close friend, Margaret Marshall, wrote about their first meeting, in 1931, not long following the publication of *American Humor*: ". . . altogether there was an air of delicacy about her, imparted by the blue and white of her eyes and hair and by the graciousness of her manner. She was friendly and warm, but essentially reserved; very much the lady, but a lady with a sense of humor. Her laughter was infectious, rich with understanding and . . . a zest for implications, wherever they might lead, that ladies in general would scarcely perceive, much less appreciate or approve of."[1]

Miss Nelle Curry, describing her visit to the Rourke home in 1940: Constance Rourke entered the room, with a tray of refreshments; "a puckish smile played around her lips." She asked whether she could move Miss Curry's chair, so that her mother, who had some difficulty hearing, could follow the conversation better. "Her smile shone on the slight, frail-looking old lady who basked in the deference always shown her by her daughter. The small room lost its bareness in the soft spotlight created by the gracious manner and the inclusive smile."[2]

Mrs. William Butler, one of her closest friends, has spoken feelingly to me, well over thirty years after Constance Rourke's death, of her warm and lovable personality. Another good friend, for almost ten years before Rourke's death—Mrs. Benjamin Merrick of Grand Rapids—has told me much the same thing. "She had a wide circle of friends here, many of them young." Miss

Rourke "was a concerned person who cared deeply about people and everything around her. Her personality gave the impression of great serenity but underneath there was fire. We all loved her."[3]

II *Figures in the Carpet*

Constance Rourke asserts in her foreword to *American Humor: A Study of the National Character* that "humor is one of those conceits which give form and flavor to an entire character." What follows suggests pretty clearly what her argument will be in the book. Comedy's relations or connections, as it "moves from a passing effervescence into the broad stream of a common possession, . . . become singularly wide." It is difficult to find a feature of our national character "to which humor is not related, few which in some sense it has not governed." Humor has made its way "into literature, not merely as an occasional touch, but as a force determining large patterns and intentions." Too, "a lawless element, full of surprises," humor "sustains its own appeal, yet its vigorous power invites absorption in that character" whose composition it enters into. Then, after commenting on the American writers' quarrel with their country or with the American character (Van Wyck Brooks, one of the most vocal critics, is not mentioned by name), Rourke points out that she is neither quarreling with the American character nor defending it. Her book derives "from an enjoyment of American vagaries," as well as from her conviction that they have formed "a tradition which is various, subtle, sinewy, scant at times but not poor."[4]

These ideas, in the light of Constance Rourke's essential beliefs (treated earlier), will help the interested reader form an understanding of the way she would develop her philosophy of American humor. This, true to Rourke's theory of popular art, will not favor comic geniuses or uniquely inspired humorists, but rather the life of the common people as they develop certain traditions and weave legends around colorful characters. The major contribution of her *American Humor*, in my opinion, is her typology: her descriptions of a number of distinctive "originals" who, as she sees them, represent the American comic spirit and show the kinds of humor that go to the root of what she called the American character. This Rourkean world of comic figures—standing for innumerable real-life performers and artists—was to be created out of the raw wilderness of eighteenth- and early-nineteenth-century America. It should be interesting to see how her mind works as she shapes this world.

Certain key terms in the passage quoted above from *American Humor* tell a great deal. To begin: Rourke's "enjoyment of American vagaries," which in her view have formed a tradition. In the first chapter of this book I discussed her commitment to the culture-philosophy of Johann Gottfried von Herder. The word "vagaries," signifying "flights of fancy" and used by Rourke to describe the raw materials of folk culture with which the artist works, opens up rich possibilities. The subject here is humor, a type of rare and beautiful bird that is too frail to survive being held in the hand and scrutinized by would-be comedian or scholar. It can withstand only the slightest bit of peering and prying: a shade too much, and it becomes a corpse—the fate of humor in the hands of practically every serious writer on the subject. Suffice it to say here that the emotional power of humor comes from its freshness and its unexpectedness, or at least a sudden severe shift in topic and tone. Hence "vagaries," suggesting a spirit of wild extravagance, puts the matter in proper perspective. And Rourke's above-quoted remark about humor being "a lawless element, full of surprises," comes to the very heart of the matter—where no investigator, unfortunately, can remain for very long.

Aside from such extremely cogent remarks as those I have just quoted, and from her essential typology of humorous American prototypes (which I shall treat shortly), Rourke's theoretical speculations about humor seem, to me, not very impressive. How far from the heart of the matter she could wander—since she was really concerned with American humor (including frontier humor and ethnic humor)—is shown in her borrowings from, and her taking quite literally, such commentators on the subject of humor as Henri Bergson and George Meredith. For example, she quotes Bergson's essay, *Laughter* (1900), to the effect that "'the comic'" makes its appearance "'just when society and the individual, freed from the worry of self-preservation, begin to regard themselves as works of art'"—and then she adds this: "With his triumphs fresh and his mind noticeably free, by 1815 the American seemed to regard himself as a work of art, and began that embellished self-portraiture which nations as well as individuals may undertake." Later in the book she cites this passage from Meredith's *Essay on*

Comedy (1877): "'a society of cultivated men and women'" must be present in order for the comic poet to arise. Such a society, where "'ideas are current and the perception quick,'" will give the comic poet "'matter and an audience.'" In her view, during that "long period out of which American comedy sprang," there was no such social milieu of gentlefolk to provide the (subject) matter, though that society might on occasion have provided the audience.[5]

I mention the matter of Rourke's strange assessments precisely at this point for two reasons. First, they occur throughout her book and thus color a number of her arguments. Second, Rourke was so bent on seeing American cultural history in terms of tradition as a unifying force, that she was led to make very sweeping and injudicious generalizations to support that point of view. This is not to say that her American comic types are particularly overdrawn, but her speaking on occasion from too little knowledge of her subject and with an excess of zeal, puts the reader on guard. The following brief examples of her incautious judgments should make this clear.

"To the primitive comic sense, to be black is to be funny," a fact taken advantage of by blackface minstrels. As the eighteenth century drew to a close, "not a tenth of the population in Kentucky had religious affiliations." (What was her source for this remarkable statistic dealing with Kentucky, admitted to the Union in 1792, two years after the first official census?) From the time of the Revolution to 1860, we may describe "American comedy" through "a series of negations." For example, it did not contain much "of the purely human." There was "no deepening of the portrayal of character, nothing of a wide and interwoven web of thought and feeling where wit might freely play and the whole be gently lighted." The dominant modes of expression of our "new American literature had remained primitive or anterior," taking the forms of "the monologue, the rhapsody, the tale, the legend, the romance." And, "full of astringencies and ellipses," they possessed a colorless tone, "archaic and young." Thus, Hawthorne, Poe, and Melville are describable "in blacks, grays, and whites," Whitman "in terms of light rather than of color." Mark Twain's "wide reach" may have great significance for a population in search of "the illusive goal of unity and the resting place of a tradition." The reason our stories during the period running from the late 1860s to the 1880s were short, was that "only a fragmentary knowledge of native life and the native character was at hand." Finally: "the novel has not developed" here; the single genuine novelist we have produced is Henry James.[6]

When she touched on the subject of Calvinism and Puritanism in relation to humor, however, she was on firmer ground; thus the reader is made to realize this fact about Rourke's commentaries on the general subject: each statement or formulation should be tested by the individual first, instead of being either accepted uncritically or rejected as another eccentric pronouncement. Thus, speaking of the Eastern seaboard area, she would point out that "emotion was stirred by the terror of the prevailing faith, yet caught within the meshwork of its tenets. Such compression with such power" would have to eventuate "in escapes and explosions." What resulted "was a rebound"; often this took place "in New England, from the time of the revelers at Merrymount onward. A constant opposition existed between the dark emotions and an earthy humor."

Then, our Revolution appeared "to set one portion of the scant population free from its narrow matrix": that is, it set free the Yankee, who sprang "clean away from the traditional faith" and who "had left the deeper emotions behind or had buried them." As proof of the Yankee's "anterior experiences" Rourke cited "his use of the mask"; this device, which would hide the pioneer's otherwise self-revealing emotions, would be his defense against the dangers he faced in his "primitive world" filled with perils. The mask was common not only among the pioneers but also "among the older Puritans as their" stronger feelings were repressed. In fact, the use of the mask had been fostered by Governor Bradford himself, who urged a number of irrepressible "spirits to enjoy themselves in secret." This mask, doubtless, would turn out to be of use "where the Puritan was still a power and the risks of pioneering" continued to be faced.[7]

The highly suggestive comments on masking are given early in the first chapter of *American Humor*, and relate directly or indirectly to all of Rourke's five basic types of comic characters, not only the type treated in that chapter. In American legend, story, stage representation, and stereotype—from the late eighteenth century through much of the nineteenth—Rourke discerns this cast of colorful performers: (1) the Yankee; (2) the gamecock of the wilderness: personified sometimes by the backwoodsman and sometimes by the boatman; (3) the Negro minstrel; (4) the strolling actor—sometimes in the figure of the revivalist; and (5) the comic poet. Whatever is left out or might be added now by way of updating, whatever overlapping may be found among the categories—Rourke is clearly at her best in the initial five chapters of the book, devoted to the above-mentioned characters and their ramifications. The four remaining chapters, containing amplifications of important points raised earlier, as well as a potpourri of related matters and further examples of American popular humor, in my opinion show a marked drop in Rourke's critical powers. Far less well organized and less cogently argued, they weaken the overall structure of the book; but more will be said about them later. Here I wish to say something about each character type as it is described in *American Humor*.

The Yankee was a shrewd rustic, a highly resourceful countryman ever ready to turn a neat homespun phrase or make an advantageous business deal; and he was colorful, somewhat inscrutable, yet admirable in a number of ways. After 1825, the Yankee plays cast him in a number of guises, each quite in harmony with the original model: "a peddler, a sailor, a Vermont wool-dealer, or merely a Green Mountain boy who traded and drawled and upset calculations"; however, he remained symbolically American, wearing his eccentric red-white-and-blue costume. "Brother Jonathan had in fact turned into Uncle Sam. Half bravado, half cockalorum," he displayed qualities that British observers found offensive: tirelessly "rural, sharp, uncouth, witty," he almost suggested a nation of peddlers, swappers, and practical jokers.[8] Parenthetically: Rourke's Yankee jokes in this section are culled from old almanacs, joke books, and other contemporary sources, discussed in her bibliographical note; and an important concern was to distinguish native American humor, wherever possible, from borrowed humor: English, classical, or whatever.

The gamecock of the wilderness was a vainglorious, obstreperous, seemingly tough old character (bantam-sized or larger), whose chief feature was his wild battle cry: a string of assertions of supernatural birth, power, prowess. "He was not only half horse, half alligator, he was also the sea-horse of the mountain, a flying whale, a bear with a sore head." He was "a steamboat, or an earthquake that shook an enemy to pieces, and he could wade the Mississippi." Names, designations, meant something to him: raccoon, "ring-tailed roarer," flower, "gamecock of the wilderness," "Salt River Roarer." Cracking his heels, "he leapt into the air to proclaim his attributes against all comers"; before "a fight he neighed like a stallion or crowed like a cock."

Often identified with the figure of the backwoodsman, the gamecock figure emerged from the War of 1812, as the Yankee had emerged from a somewhat earlier war, the American Revolution. His wild shouting might have covered an inner insecurity relating to the possession of power and size, which concerned him so intensely. Too, there appeared to be a self-intoxicating effect on the gamecock-backwoodsman from this shouting, which was ritualistic, suggesting that he might gain from it all that he claimed in the way of superior qualities. When he did engage in a fighting match, after the appropriate boasts and bluster, he might have been attempting (like some savage ritualist) "to create strength for the tribe by exhibiting strength." Although life was precarious in the wilds, he retained "a comic oblivious tone"; disdaining the risks of his wilderness existence, he could manage to remain cheerful.

The other type of gamecock of the wilderness was the boatman: the robust and intrepid trader, freight handler, roustabout, explorer, working the waterways of the American interior in the East and Midwest by means of canoe, flatboat, keelboat. "The boatman blew his magic horn," says Rourke after a beautiful lyric passage about life on the Ohio River in spring (and after quoting four stanzas of a boatman's song), "and improvised sentimental songs." Pulling on his oar, "he slipped into a highly posed melancholy," growing "elegiac over lost loves."

Since Rourke was so intent on bringing in, whenever she could, gigantic hero-figures of popular legend and lore, she would cite Davy Crockett ("hunter and backwoods oracle") as the exemplar of the first subtype of the gamecock, and Mike Fink ("the first flatboatman . . . to take a broadhorn over the Falls of the Ohio") as the exemplar of the second subtype. Different in certain basic ways, the backwoodsman and the boatman, in the flesh and in the popular imagination, had much in common: ethnic origin (generally Scotch or English); desire for isolation; musical tastes and preferences. Each enjoyed lively dancing, and mixed "Negro breakdowns with Irish reels and jigs. . . . Comic resilience swept through them in waves, transcending the past, transcending terror, with the sense of comedy." Boasting and rhapsodizing, they "made a rising clamor in the forests and along the great rivers." But then again they might suddenly fall silent; they had "the thirsty curiosity of the backwoods." These gun-carrying men of the wilds, like other frontiersmen, had "a gift for masquerade"; their faces were blank. And, they "were fond of costume, wearing bright fringes and many-colored coats."[9]

The Negro minstrel was originally a creation of white showmen and entertainers, such as Edwin Forrest and Thomas ("Jim Crow") Rice, in the early 1800s, although Negro performers had been on the stage at least a generation earlier. The white Negroes exaggerated the mannerisms of plantation laborers, Negro dandies, and other familiar Negro types: for comic effect. Rice popularized an old Negro dance-song, "Jim Crow," and made himself up as a blackface Yankee dressed in "red and white striped trousers and long blue coat"; the latter garment was celebrated in one of Rice's most successful numbers, "That Long-tail'd Blue," which described the tribulations suffered by the coat's wearer. Here Rice was in effect impersonating a Negro impersonating a white. Not long after, he "took off" various Negro stereotypes; then he created an innovative "Ethiopian opera"; a rousing blackface song-and-dance sequence. So popular was Rice's new theatrical form in America during the 1830s and the following decade, that he went with it to London, where he was also enormously successful.

What Rourke calls Negro minstrelsy (i.e., the Negro minstrel show) dates from 1842. In that year four white men—three Yankees led by a backwoodsman named Dan Emmett, who resembled "a Yankee deacon"—put on a words-music-and-dance performance in blackface, their instruments four in number: tambo, bones, banjo, and fiddle. According to Emmett, all of the performers were interlocutors just as all were end-men. Each was dressed in "that long-tail'd blue." At the center of the show there was singing by the ensemble; "in its wake came larger numbers in the choral dancing of the walkaround."

On the subject of the songs and dances of the Negro minstrel (who might actually have been white), Rourke suggestively refers to Negro roots and white composition. Dan Emmett's "Ole Dan Tucker," for example, had a number of distinctive Negro features, one of them being the "brief and cryptic bird and animal fables" allegorizing: (1) the Negro's hunted and degraded state, and (2) his ability to outwit his persecutors. Emmett had long been directly exposed to Negro life, and even worked together with Thomas ("Jim Crow") Rice over a period of time; yet, steeped as he was in

Negro folk materials, and prominent as those were in his songs (as well as in "his walkarounds and choruses"), he would have it that he wrote those songs himself. A number of them, actually, bore a marked resemblance to Negro spirituals, from which Stephen Foster drew a good bit of his inspiration.

Rourke traces the walkaround (which featured "competitive dancing in the mazes of a circle") to the dances of the Negro slaves on the plantations, and ultimately to African tribal dances. But her basic concern is to treat what is essentially American about such a folk-art form as the minstrel show. Thus she sees "Negro minstrelsy [as having] arisen from the Southwest and from Negro life there; it showed many traces of regional origins." Moreover, "Western myth-making was woven deep in early minstrelsy," to such an extent that it is difficult to consider it a foreign element. There was even an Irish influence here, as far as jigs, reels, and tunes were concerned: Negroes apparently learned the "musical idiom" of the Irish easily. Still, Rourke leaves the strong impression that in spite of the Irish component or that of the "English contradance," and in spite of the fact that "the persistent stress was primitive," the Negro minstrel was, and ought to be considered, a homegrown American product.[10]

Perhaps the stock character of the strolling actor in Rourke's presentation (which deals primarily with country or backwoods theater) does not come through quite as well as the earlier types do, She herself shows that the Yankee, the backwoodsman, and the Negro minstrel were popular stage figures as well as actual folk types; this does not sharpen categorical distinctions. In trying to delineate the strolling actor in his secular form, she indicates that in her view he was concerned not so much with serious drama as with theatricals: by which she means improvisations, special comic and burlesque routines, startling stage effects. Thus she can say of our drama that "as a powerful native form [it] did not appear in America" in the early years of the Republic, nor did it in the course of the last century. "But the theatrical seemed a native mode." The latter would appeal to the rustic, credulous audiences she describes as entering intimately into, and taking as reality, the stories presented on the rough, back-country stages. Retaining some of the deeper feelings of the earlier pioneers (sensitivity to supernatural forces and to man's conflicts with the elements), those untutored folk, so susceptible to exaggerated histrionics, responded in different ways to two familiar stage roles. The

Indian was a tragic, noble savage of romance: homeless and ill-used, but exalted because he lived next to unspoiled nature. But the soldier-hero of the Revolutionary War was often made into a figure of fun when he was considered at all for a stage role.

It is not surprising that, under the circumstances, the strolling actors, in choosing what kinds of shows to put on, "swung into comedy as if under the direction of a popular impulse." Serious emotion was repressed or kept on a superficial level. The theater did not offer its supporters a "humanly comprehensive" appeal: "The lyric sweep was never included, the passion of love never revealed." And the darker emotions were pitched so high that they could readily break apart.

In fact, as Rourke would have it, a form related to comedy—burlesque—took over the stage in the 1840s and 1850s, "turning the serious drama upsidedown, and joining with the comic [trio of] the Yankee, the backwoodsman, and the Negro minstrel." Among the reasons Rourke gives for the virtual discontinuance of the legitimate theater (which made possible the spread of burlesque)—the vogue of dancing, the popularity of public lectures, the burning of New York's National Theater, etc.—one in particular bears on the character of the strolling actor. "Vicissitudes which naturally beset actors in a rude country furthered the movement into burlesque." And she cites the case of an actor playing a tragic hero, and falling "in death with part of his body extended off stage so that he might play his own death music on the fiddle." A part "of the audience," she observes, "was bound to see the double accomplishment." She discusses burlesque operas and gives amusing excerpts from popular burlesque plays such as John Brougham's *Pocahontas* and *Columbus el Filibustero*. However, Rourke confusingly does not always maintain the distinction between the rough-and-ready country theater and the professional theater in a city such as New York.

As a result of Rourke's emphasis on burlesque productions for both the rural and the urban stage, the strolling actor (as I have said) is not sharply enough defined. Her vagueness on this point is mirrored in a remark she makes about backwoods dramatics. "By their own wish and in the fancy of their audiences these people of the theater remained a caste apart." Old superstitions may have played a part in this: the black arts and the machinations of the devil were suggested by the changes taking place on the stage.[11]

Then there were the clerical strollers, whom Rourke also

regarded as actors of a sort: millenarians, revivalists, cultists. They "belonged to the theater"; like their secular counterpart they assumed an underlying romantic outlook; and, "they moved toward comedy, [and] burlesque." Here she may have been drawing on such wildly irreverent frontier humorists as G.W. Harris (creator of Sut Lovingood) and J.J. Hooper (creator of Simon Suggs), both of whom she cites in her bibliographical note. But she treats the culture patterns they describe, with all the roguish preachers and all the scandalous carryings on at camp meetings, as deriving from a post-Calvinist religious temper.

Emotionally volatile, and of a strong religious heritage, these crude backwoods folk threw off their restraints and yielded themselves up (for the moment at least) to the magnetic power of some self-appointed Interpreter of the Word. There were "orgiastic forest revivals" with the participants "shouting and pleading to be bathed in the blood of the Lamb, and bending, writhing, jerking, falling, barking, and creeping over the ground like the creatures of the wilderness." The bucolic revivals, with their stylized baptisms and confessions of faith, their performing strollers and singers, signified (to Constance Rourke at least) that "a rude and violent form of the divine comedy" was being acted out.

The reason for her choice of the term "divine comedy," which has some bearing on her character type of the clerical stroller (actor), is as follows. "Comedy" to her—as to Dante, whose *Divina Commedia* is somehow suggested here—presupposed a joyous, desirable ending: the opposite of what was to be found in "tragedy." Now, she saw Calvinism as "profoundly dramatic" because it involved "inner conflicts and [a] cataclysmic formula of the human relation to God"; man was the lowest object on earth but with God's eternal anger directed against him, he "gained stature." However, the newly fashioned religious movements of the day moved ever further away from Calvinism's "strict and sober drama," although they retained this important dramatic feature of the latter: the element of terror, deriving from the emphasis on death, and from those "prolonged anxieties" preceding spiritual peace. Rather than favoring narrow doctrines, those sects inclined toward such features as "improvisation, rapturous climaxes, happy assurances, and a choral strain." In their religious revivals (led, as experience has shown, by spellbinding performers) were to be found rhapsody and monologue—in the form of witnessing, for example; and from the monologue would come fantasy. This "wildly hopeful" mode of expression in the sects and cults of the 1830s and 1840s, Rourke treats in terms of comedy, albeit religious comedy. And she generalizes as follows on Brigham Young's introducing "theatricals" but forbidding tragedy among his long-suffering Mormon followers, once they arrived in Utah: he followed a prevailing pattern "within American attitudes, . . . flight away from oppressive circumstance into comedy."[12]

Constance Rourke's chapter on the comic poet is, I feel, the weakest of her first five chapters, dealing with the comic character types. Aside from its vague generalizations and the arguable literary judgments (mentioned earlier), it does not really define the comic poet, and the relevant background material that should help clarify this nebulous character contains discrepancies. An example follows.

Early in the chapter Rourke refers to the "simple and legendary outline" by means of which amusing characters were drawn—for (among other reasons) depiction on the stage and storytelling purposes: the Irish boy and girl, the riffraff New York "'b'hoy,'" and other assorted ethnic types. Then she relates these comic stereotypes to her "comic trio": Yankee, backwoodsman, Negro— because of certain characteristics supposedly held in common, such as humble origin and societal scorn. No mention here of the fourth comic stereotype, the stroller, who in his secular, stage-entertainer form, might have been represented as a Yankee, a backwoodsman, a Negro, or some combination of those. Yet there is another incongruity in Rourke's summary of the underlying comic elements of American literature—which presumably would nourish our comic poets. At the end of the chapter, speaking of those who provided a substratum for our literature, she specifies: (1) Yankees, (2) "[backwoodsmen] in minstrelsy"—whose influence was not as direct, (3) theatrical strollers, and cultist and revivalist strollers, and (4) "the innumerable comic story-tellers and myth-makers." This time the Negro is left out of consideration.

The one remote candidate for comic poet in this chapter is Abraham Lincoln, whose reputation as a storyteller endeared him to Constance Rourke. Through her attributing to him a number of humorous qualities and roles, the reader may finally get some idea, however vague, of what is comical and yet poetic about the hypothesized comic poet, the fifth and last stereotype in *American*

Humor's major gallery of portraits. Lincoln's conversation was a point of departure for any number of stories, which yielded "a hardy comic poetry . . . [now] part of a popular lore." In his narratives Lincoln made use of our "entire native strain" as he sustained the roles of "actor, . . . mimic, caricaturist," as well as "maker of burlesque." He apparently combined "two of the larger strains of American comedy"; one strain was "the western ebullience" and the other involved an ancestral Yankee influence. There was "earthy poetry" in his stories; he employed "the fable, the allegory, the tale grounded in metaphor." All of which suggest, not the rhymed sentiments of the conventional and ordinary poet, but rather—among other, more general "poetic" qualities— colorful turn of phrase, special rhythm of delivery, and a keen sense of the dramatic. Nevertheless, Rourke's quoted examples of Lincoln's stories and attempts at ridicule appear more heavy-handed than even mildly humorous, in the 1980s.

As Rourke views our earlier history, the period from the American Revolution up to 1860, we failed to produce a comic poet from the populace at large, though there was a wealth of "comic poetry" and it retained the "archetypal largeness" inherent "in the more elementary poetic forms." During this eighty-five-year time-span, there was no "fertilizing contact between new and old," yet "the comic spirit" was always making its way "into new areas." Here as elsewhere in the chapter, Rourke's vagueness and generalizing tendency are made to carry the burden of her argument. What "archetypal largeness" is intended? What "new areas"? The "largest movement" of our "comic poetry" was, according to her, in the direction of "the epical, the heroic," even "the mock heroic on the epical scale." And since the comic stereotypes depicted in the first half of *American Humor* represent the old areas, those "new areas" would represent a wider range of individualized assertions of our comic spirit: in forms such as monologue, tale, rhapsody.

That Rourke would go on in the next chapter ("I Hear America Singing") to call these and two related forms (legend and romance) "prevailing forms of the new American literature [that] had remained primitive or anterior"[13] suggests this. *American Humor* is thus a rather confusing book. Something else suggests this also, and it makes the text all the more challenging for the serious reader. The comic stereotypes, not always designated consistently, represent our literature's "groundwork": i.e., the old elements in it. But looked at another way they are not old, insofar as their subsequent adaptations will be treated in the latter half of *American Humor*, along with certain other new materials.

III *Sweeping Up*

The remaining four chapters of Rourke's book—"I Hear America Singing"; "Facing West From California's Shores"; "The American"; "Round Up"—are considerably less organized than even her rambling and diffuse "Comic Poet" chapter. Instead of attempting to untangle completely the snarl of latter-day comic stereotypes, and quasi-humorous forms (monologue, tale, rhapsody, legend, romance), I shall try to give a little of the "sense" of this portion of *American Humor* by suggesting an overview and by selecting certain relevant and emblematic details.

Just as humor is so vaguely (if provocatively) defined in this book that almost any writer may turn up here as some kind of humorist (though certain amusing writers are unaccountably left out)—Rourke treats another important mode of expression as though it too were a common tendency. This mode is poetry, and if allowance is made for lilting, rhapsodic prose, for emotion-charged but nonmetrical literary expression, Rourke's thesis about this important adjunct to humor becomes easier to accept. But is this quite what Rourke intends, in her sweeping emphasis on poetry, that will first relegate the comic-poet stereotype of our earlier history to a modest position among other, more striking stereotypes, and then reverse the scale of importance in the comic poet's favor? The answer is: not precisely. To get a more exact idea of her meaning of poetry, which informs so much of *American Humor*, it is necessary to look more closely at her actual statements.

Speaking of our native American theater in the 1850s, Rourke would see it as fairly out of touch with real life, having as "its medium . . . a rude and incompleted [*sic*] poetry. Even its portraiture belonged to . . . a broad and experimental comic poetry." At one point a specific statement is finally made about the poetic mode. This is in connection with her remark concerning the years between the American Revolution and 1860: during which time there was no comic poet, though we had comic poetry. The latter, developed on numerous levels (not only the folk level), retained its "archetypal largeness . . ., with the inevitable slide into figure and that compact turn with unspoken implications which is the essence of poetic expression." At the beginning of her "Round Up" chapter, Rourke generalizes: "The pattern created for an American literature had been touched with poetry" repeatedly and in fact "had often been grounded in a primitive poetry." American literature's "first modern approaches to character and the native scene" were made—not in the form of the novel—but in the form of poetry. And, although "narrative . . . [in America] has at least verged toward the poetical, . . . its poetry is not yet a poetry of contemporary life."

I do not wish, here, to refute these colossal, peremptory generalizations that must keep the serious reader of *American Humor* ever on the alert. Among these strange judgments, in fact, other surprises may be found. For example, the idea that "the novel has not developed in America." Or, the notion that "American expression has always moved toward the theatrical or the dramatic." But what requires attention is Rourke's intense concern with the poetical mode in this particular book. Though she never wrote any poetry, so far as I am aware, she would nevertheless idealize it in the abstract, defining it almost out of recognition. And, aided by such a definition (which was not at odds with her philosophy of aesthetics and folk art), she would then find this poetry—with its comic concomitants—in happy abundance throughout our literature. Her touchstones in this definition, which takes in "the more elementary poetic forms" as well as "the essence of poetic expression," are just different enough (however slight the difference) from what most commentators on poetry would suggest, to bear a little explication.[14]

The three significant elements, indicated above, are: "archetypal largeness," "the inevitable slide into figure" (i.e., figure of speech: metaphor, simile, hyperbole, etc.), and "that compact turn with unspoken implications." In sum: a getting away from things-as-they-are and a moving into a special land of make-believe. Not the ordinary realm of the imagination that poetry is supposed to open up to the reader, not an idealized "better" world where truth and beauty are equivalent or where all earthly, personal wrongs are made right, but rather, a Rourkean world of rare and thrilling splendor. Heroic giants have left their impress here, though they are not actually seen any longer. In fact, things in general may look much bigger than normal, as they do in western tall tales. If the Paul Bunyans and Davy Crocketts of legend are not now in evidence, other colorful types are: (1) rip-snorting, language-bending gamecocks of the wilderness, and (2) evasive Yankees protecting themselves through double-talk or laconic grunts. Now and then the influence of the Negro and of the strolling actor or revivalist will be felt too: the Negro, with his code language based on ancestral folk patterns and social or private protest against his American ordeal; the stroller, with his dissembling in speech and dress. On occasion certain of these character types might even coalesce. This other "world out of a wilderness" then is Rourke's world of poetry, the "supreme fiction" she herself has made in her mind, from the offerings of her native culture and her physical environment. With its "lawless, surprising elements" and its vagaries, it is a comic world too.

And so the latter portion of *American Humor* deals extensively—but by no means exclusively—with actual poets: Walt Whitman, Emily Dickinson, Edwin A. Robinson, Vachel Lindsay, Robert Frost, Edgar Lee Masters, and Carl Sandburg. Whitman is seen as a kind of gamecock of the wilderness sounding his barbaric yawp, reflecting "the spirit of American popular comedy," moving on an epic scale although the heroic was generally beyond him. This wildly boasting, rhapsodic backwoodsman from Long Island and Brooklyn—nature's child—celebrated his "spontaneous self"and "turned the native comic [backwoods] rhapsody . . . to broad poetic forms." He even developed themes that might have been taken from the strolling revivalists, and announced—as some of them did—that he intended to found a new religion. Dickinson, who was "in a profound sense a comic poet in the American tradition," had "the sense of scale" (that is, a distinctive notion of relative size of physical objects). This was exemplified by her "little tippler leaning against the sun" and "purple mountains moving" poems, mentioned among others by Rourke. Moreover, Dickinson's poems were "comic in the Yankee strain, with its resilience and sudden unprepared ironical lines."

Edwin A. Robinson populated his legendary Tilbury Town with "types recurrent throughout early American comedy": marginal characters in society, misfits. He commanded an "unobtrusive Yankee irony"; a Yankee speech style may be discerned in his blank verse. Burlesque and "understated comedy" are also present in his writing. Just as character was Robinson's "great subject"and fantasy "his genuine subject," tragedy was "his great theme": a

"groundwork of defeat" for all his Miniver Cheevys and Richard
Corys. But Robinson's brand of tragedy was balanced by the
barely noticeable "reticent humor" to be found in his poems.

Here, in her section on Robinson, Rourke reiterates with special
application her Herderian view of folk tradition and art: "only
when traditions are deeply established [can] a whole literature . . .
be created." And she observes a definite change in our national
literature, with its recently developed solidity and breadth—
judging from the work of the four poets with whom she grouped
Robinson: Masters, Frost, Lindsay, Sandburg. Their writings
show "characters, fantasies, and patterns of mind or feeling"
which may be seen "in an early comic folk-lore." In Masters's
Spoon River Anthology "humor is turned to irony and joined with
. . . tenderness"; the "basic living speech" (found in Whitman and
some of these other poets) comes "from a race of talkers and oral
story-tellers." Brief though the individual speeches are, again we
find "the legendary scale" (E. A. Robinson's studies of character
treated its "legendary aspects"). And once more, Masters followed
the patterns of "popular comedy" and our "early literature" in
emphasizing the character of the communal group, such as the
village.

Frost's speech patterns reveal to Rourke "familiar Yankee
rhythms, unobtrusive and slow"; his drawing of character is done
in the customary Yankee manner, generally "with an indirect
beginning, scant emphasis, a slow unraveling." She finds Frost
retaining a "native humor," which frequently intensifies "to a
bitter irony"; the greater part of Frost's humor is almost inextrica-
ble from his speech—as was the case with humor and speech
patterns in "the early Yankee tradition." With regard to Sandburg
too, Rourke responds to the way in which the words may be
spoken aloud: in his "poetry . . . speech is dominant, taking free
poetic forms"; reading his poetry will reduce its effect. As with
Whitman, Sandburg's material is often improvised, representing
notes for what might later become poems—yet his "rhythms are
his own," coming as they do "from the speech of a late day and a
mixed people." Sandburg's poetry of America—its geography and
topography—is permeated with "an exhilarated, inflated humor"
that is of "the West," with a simpler exuberant humor, or with "a
simple irony." Once more, Rourke is struck by the poet's "sense of
scale"; Sandburg's is a bit mischievous. Rourke compares it with
John James Audubon's "sense of scale" in this regard, and quotes

Sandburg's "Many Hats," with its bluejays tweeting out "'Another lovely morning,'" after people have died in race riots. And, Sandburg used the rhapsody (very much of an American mode), and expressed "communal rather than individual emotion."

As for Vachel Lindsay: "a latter-day gamecock of the wilderness" with an occasional "genteel cast" and "a primitive nationalistic feeling." Belligerent, noisy, and crude as he evokes our cultural legacy, he suggests to Rourke "a throwback to some of the earlier [nineteenth-century] comedians." Like our "earlier comic poets" he has attempted to shape his own myths (for example, "Bryan" and "General Booth Enters into Heaven"). He bespeaks our "early fabulous era," possessing the endless "good humor" and inconsistent "air of surprise" associated with that era. Lindsay's poetry reveals "a wild comic fantasy" reflecting that "extravagant oral style of the past." Frequently "oratorical, theatrical, evangelical," Lindsay "overflows with the exuberant story-telling of the West."[15]

Before leaving the matter of Rourke's treatment of poetry and the broad applications of her comic-poet stereotype, it is necessary to touch on a few points by way of summary comment. First, there is her emphasis on "sense of scale" or "legendary scale." This in her system of thought relates to the "archetypal largeness" mentioned earlier in the reference to her "essence of poetic expression." Second, in her remarks on all the poets cited above, Rourke is concerned with living speech in various modes and styles: Yankee speech, ironic speech, rhapsodic speech, etc. This strong response to the elements of voice and diction in poetry has to do with the other above-mentioned elements in the "essence of poetic expression": figurative language, and what she calls the "compact turn with unspoken implications." Third, it is worth remembering that Rourke's "comic poet" may well take other guises, particularly those of Yankee and backwoodsman. Thus the "comic poet" figure, so poorly depicted in the chapter devoted to him in *American Humor,* and presented so much more forcefully in the later chapters, almost becomes an embodiment of American comic humor.

Fourth and last. Aside from all of Rourke's comments in her book, what were her actual contacts, if any, with the world of poetry? Nelle Curry's biographical essay has a word on this. Writing in 1930 from the MacDowell Colony in Peterborough, New Hampshire (the recipient of the letter is not named), Rourke

mentioned that Edwin Arlington Robinson, who was at the artists'
colony each summer, was currently in residence. Though Robinson had for a long period been "'abysmally shy,'" at this time, aged
sixty, he had become quite loquacious. Presently he was "'in a very
mellow mood.'" She added the rumor that Robinson's new disposition was due to the fact that his book *Tristram* (1927) had been so
well received by the public. This led her to remark that she
happened "'to know that it started before that, for he occasionally
talked whole paragraphs when I was here six years ago.'" Back in
Grand Rapids, she met with a little coterie "'to read their favorite
poems to each other'"; her contribution was Elinor Wylie's poetry.
(Note: considering the extreme irregularity of that bohemian
lady's life, and Constance Rourke's deeply ingrained decorousness,
it is interesting that she chose the Wylie poems.) Another contemporary poet whom she regarded very highly was Léonie Adams,
and she praised certain of Joseph Auslander's poems: one to Elinor
Wylie, another to Amy Lowell.[16] All of which indicates something
about Rourke's aesthetic range: she could also respond to poets of
her own time, who might not reflect a comic view of things,
"archetypal largeness," or distinctive speech patterns.

Other comic stereotypes, while they often seem projections of
Rourke's "comic poet," are granted a small amount of space in the
latter chapters of *American Humor*, where they are treated
fleetingly on their own terms. In scattered references, the figure of
the Yankee is presented to us through the writings of such authors
as Emerson, Thoreau, Melville, Henry James (who was
"grounded in the Yankee fable"), and E. A. Robinson. The stroller
is exemplified in, for example, Artemus Ward, Petroleum V.
Nasby, and Orpheus C. Kerr; Ward, the most accomplished of the
group "in the sheer comedy of sound, used the Yankee speech with
an overlay from the backwoods and called the product Hoosier."
The gamecock is seen, as I have indicated, in Walt Whitman—
placed by Rourke with the backwoodsmen contingent—and also
in Mark Twain, who is included with both the backwoodsmen and
the riverboatmen; Twain is also placed in the Yankee category and
the briefly mentioned (outside) category of the Californian.

Rourke appears very interested, in these latter chapters, in
certain generic expressions of humor or near-humor—monologue,
tale, rhapsody, legend, romance—which cut across the blurred
comic-stereotype groupings and allow her sufficient scope to touch
on certain special aspects of the comic spirit. These are apt to be

overlooked by an insensitive commentator on humor, concerned with matters Rourke does not stress: slapstick, farce, ridicule through mimicry and pantomime, etc. In that above-mentioned series, to be looked at briefly now, monologue—sometimes referred to by Rourke as soliloquy—is by far the most important, and I shall save it for the last. There will be a good deal of overlapping of categorical types here too, but distinctions may still conveniently be drawn.

An idea of how neatly Rourke could bring together important features of her philosophy of American culture and her theory of American humor, may be gained from a look at one of her references to the generic modes (tale, etc.). The bold Rourkean network of influences and forms suddenly reveals itself from a welter of ensnarled observations on Herman Melville's *Moby-Dick*. She begins with the notion of largeness—the hero, the epic—and moves outward. "The heroic outline had" already been suggested, "in popular comedy as on the levels of literature." John James Audubon, in his *Birds of America* and other works, was not far from "the epical form." A number of fiction writers: Fenimore Cooper, R. M. Bird, W. G. Simms, D. P. Thompson, and J. P. Kennedy, working carefully through our heritage of the past, "used a scope that roughly approached the epical scale." Their stories went back to the uncomplicated, "cumulative" narrative forms of "the popular stories of the taverns and the almanacs: these were tales." Linked together, the tales would become narrative cycles, "not novels but romances," with something out of the ordinary, as Hawthorne had recommended. "Legends were striated through them," as well as particles of myth. They dealt with frontier experience—"their living characters were comic: scouts, bee-hunters, horse-thieves, wandering ne'er-do-wells, Negroes." W. G. Simms's tales were the first to present a full-length picture of the Negro. R. M. Bird made use of "western comic talk and character."

Again: that particular reference both separates and jumbles together some of Rourke's generic modes (tale, legend, romance) and comic-stereotype figures. As she discusses the tale, in Poe, Hawthorne, and Mark Twain, she clarifies somewhat just what she means by this loose term and indicates how the tale and related genres express the subtler, less-obvious aspects of the comic spirit in America. And, as her book is designed to show, it is that spirit, embodied in our cultural tradition, that is one of the important facets of our national character, as well as a unifying force for our diverse ethnic and racial populations. Now the tale, in Rourke's references to it, appears as a lively narrative of unusual events, told with the idea of affecting the audience in some way. The action proper is not confined to the tale's plot, but is also expressed in the psychological changes in the teller and the listeners. She refers pointedly to the popular (often comic) story-tellers in our country inns, in the theaters, or wherever strangers got together. And she makes much of Mark Twain's 1897 essay, "How to Tell a Story," with its famous spook tale of the dead wife's golden arm: a tale Twain recommended for scaring the wits out of a frightened girl in the back of the auditorium. Pertinently, she mentions Twain's contrasting three kinds of stories on the basis of national preference. "'The humorous story is American'"; it "'depends for its effect upon the *manner* of telling.'" Thus did Twain define "the native quality . . . he had made his own"; Twain's "stories were oral and histrionic: manner was everything."

It is significant that Rourke makes emotion an important part of the tale. The emotion may be openly expressed through "manner of story-telling" as well as through contents, or it may be provocatively suppressed, as in the case of Hawthorne. Successive readings of her book will show that her subtle insistence on feeling, through a wide range of emotional effects—though she does intellectualize too—gives her philosophy of American humor its strange power. "Since feeling *is* first" with her (Cummings's poem has relevance here), the readings will also help explain why she is inclined to treat so many seemingly unhumorous writers as exemplars of the American comic spirit. Conversely, something additional may at least be suggested: how she could overlook so many writers, and familiar writings of cited authors, that do reflect American humor. So then, her remarks about emotion in the tales of Poe and Hawthorne will help provide a framework for her treatment of the other quasi-humorous genres: legend, romance, rhapsody, monologue.

Poe, keenly attuned to contemporary objects of interest, "turned to comedy. . . [and] to the hoax." What he aimed for here "was to make his readers absurd," imbecilic. He sought for "triumph, the familiar objective of popular comedy." And his characters (in the "burlesques and extravaganzas") were distorted beyond recognition, as he made use of a "grotesquerie . . . [lying] midway between the comic and the terrible." Poe also employed "the magnified scale" to describe interiors, details of decor, sensations. He delighted in mystifying his readers; everywhere his "tone and level . . . were those of legend"; again, he would project "black moods and emotions," encompassing "a dark and ghostly melodrama."

Unlike Poe, with his penchant for horror, terror, and the grotesque (as they shade into a bizarre kind of comedy), Hawthorne dealt with arrested emotion: "rage, greed, terror, the sense of guilt—are only half lighted." Rourke mentions Dimmesdale's concealment of his relationship to Hester, in *The Scarlet Letter*, as an example of this emotional inhibition. And she cogently points up Hawthorne's strong concern (in his "briefer tales") over the Unpardonable Sin, "the sin against the heart." But—so runs Rourke's logic—not only was emotion diminished in Hawthorne, but scope as well, and Rourke points out that Hawthorne's narratives, whether long or short, had the tale's "brief scope." Yet one additional element was attenuated in his writings, and this enabled Rourke to bring in other generic modes besides the tale.

Her reasoning is as follows. Hawthorne did not know what actual people, among whom he lived, were really like; our "native character" had been examined only in travelers' superficial sketches, in "prototypal drawings." Because of this Hawthorne moved in the direction of legend, which the "native impulse of comedy" was helping to form in the American mind. And it was legend, in her definition, that allowed "a fantastic or narrow or generalized handling of character." This is an important state-ment, which will have a bearing on a number of Rourke's interests, including comic stereotypes of our culture (Yankee, backwoodsman, stroller, etc.), the epic (or magnified) scale, folklore giants such as Paul Bunyan or Davy Crockett, and folk or popular art. Looking for characters "odd and salient," Hawthorne frequently treated them humorously in his notebooks, inflating and caricaturing them. He regarded *The House of the Seven Gables* as a romance and in this connection wished to include the flavor of "the Marvellous" and to be free to ignore verisimilitude. He considered the story (Hawthorne also used the word "tale") to be a legend linking the past with the present, conveying from the former "'some of its legendary mist.'" Rourke sees another of his books, *The Scarlet Letter*, and Hawthorne's "finer work" in general as having "the bold and poetic and legendary outline" possessed by opera. From legend to fable. (One definition of fable in the 1976 *American Heritage Dictionary*: "A story about legendary persons and exploits.") To Rourke, Henry James's *The American*, with its American innocence versus European experience (and duplicity), its "large, generic, American character"—Christopher Newman—its satire, is "the complete fable," in which innocence does not triumph.

It has been necessary to quote at some length from Rourke, in order to give the sense of her arguments. Tale, legend, romance, distort their subject matter—compressing and twisting here, inflating and enlarging there. In these types of departure from reality Rourke, apparently, detects the spirit of comedy, the strand of American humor that is part of our national character. Parenthetically: since we lacked a society of cultivated gentlefolk during our early period, Rourke could not apply George Meredith's criterion for the "comic poet" (by extension, for comedy itself), to eighteenth- and nineteenth-century America: she was obliged to shape her own criteria. This may be another reason why her judgments on what is humorous or comic in any way seem curious, with unlikely inclusions and glaring omissions. For instance, in regard to rhapsody (extremely enthusiastic expression of feeling), Rourke cites "The rhapsodic, leaping, crowing backwoodsman," mentions Whitman in this connection, and twice refers to Melville's *Moby-Dick*. Finding comedy very much in evidence in that great whaling narrative, she feels that its "movement . . . is that of comic travesty"; soaring and circling, it "rises to the persistent native form of rhapsody."

Just at this point, though, her sensitivity becomes more acute than normal and she pulls a number of observations together to make a provocative and penetrating argument. In *Moby-Dick* Melville projected "sardonic humor," and revealed the "terror and sense of evil and impending death" that had frequently been found in our "comic legends." Penetrating "comedy's mask" in search of "its ultimate secret," Melville included in his novel the epic's necessary "final element . . . an encounter between gods and men." Thus Rourke moves beyond her subtle argument involving humor-through-distortion of character or event, to the less humorous distortion of emotion (in rhapsody), to the tragic outer reaches of comedy, to the cosmic implications of the great epics, wherein there is a human confrontation with the divine. (Melville's Ahab—"a prototypical figure"—enters into a "titanic and inhuman struggle" with another prototypical figure, the great white whale: the embodiment of all the evil in the universe.) But Rourke's treatment of that remaining quasi-humorous genre—monologue or soliloquy—deserves special attention, I feel, for it is one of the distinctive features of *American Humor*, once we allow for the major importance of the essential stereotypes: Yankee, gamecock of the wilderness, stroller, Negro, comic poet.

This voicing of the exploration of one's inner mind, soliloquizing for the benefit of an audience or of the self or both, is actually made so much of by Rourke, that a big question arises. Is she using it as an umbrella to cover most instances of American humor? Put another way: allowing for Rourke's ideas concerning American humor—"vagaries," "lawless element, full of surprises," the sketching of particular character types, etc.—is she not suggesting that the monologue, more than any other generic form or embodiment of humor, can put these things into practice? On closer analysis this turns out not to be the case. Her monologue is no omnium gatherum. Despite Rourke's long list of monologists and soliloquizers—among them: Poe, Emerson, Thoreau, Hawthorne, Melville, Whitman, Artemus Ward, Mark Twain, Bret Harte, Henry James (i.e., certain of his female characters), Edwin A. Robinson, Robert Frost, Edgar Lee Masters, Finley Peter Dunne, Ring Lardner, Eugene O'Neill (for example, *Strange Interlude*), Sherwood Anderson ("I'm A Fool"), Sinclair Lewis—a certain pattern emerges that transcends monologue and has important affinities with other of Rourke's generic forms of humor. This pattern will lead us back, not only to Rourke's overall view of American humor, but to her philosophy of popular culture and the production of art.

As Rourke treats the monologue or soliloquy, through all of these writers and a host of unnamed full- or part-time humorists (including newspaper columnists), a scale of measurement may be discerned. This has nothing to do with her frequently mentioned "epic scale," which is related (in her thinking) with the substance and heroes of legend. Rather, it concerns the individual, probing his own mind to its depths and allowing his thought processes free rein: the individual who may be measured, very generally, according to his degree of social interaction. At one extreme the individual under consideration may be important because he is a "solitary" in his own make-do world of ideas. At the other extreme the individual may represent an extended social group with its

ongoing tradition and system of folkways. Somewhere in between
these two, the writer Rourke takes up for brief consideration may
be thinking out loud from the recesses of his private world, but
carefully regulating what he says according to the subtle changes
in his social group: his audience. Taken together, those three types
of monologists, embodying to a certain extent and also transcending Rourke's groupings discussed in the preceding pages, give a fair
idea (as I have indicated above) of what *American Humor: A
Study of the National Character* is all about.

Poe's penetration into his own subconscious, described through
a first-person narrative style, led to certain important, possibly
even humorous, discoveries (or rediscoveries) about the self.
Rourke subtly hints more than once in her book, that this kind of
delving—recall her references to "American vagaries" and humor
being "a lawless element, full of surprises"—holds rich psychological possibilities. Her remarks on Poe and her direct quotations in
this regard, are especially interesting. In "The Black Cat" he
dealth with "'the spirit of PERVERSENESS,'" for example the soul's
"'unfathomable longing . . . *to vex itself*—to offer violence to its
own nature.'" In "Ligeia" he took up the problem of memory, of
remaining merely on "'*the very verge* of remembrance.'" "William Wilson" presents—through the complicated but obscure
workings of memory—the theme of the individual divided against
himself. And, in summing up Poe's modus operandi, free as it was
from Puritan influence, from moral concerns, Rourke touches on
one of the trademarks of American humor of whatever subtype,
the deadpan, though she does not name it. Poe resembles the
Western tale-spinners telling "with blank and undisturbed counte-
nances" about "wild and perverse actions," narrators whose insistence on "the first person brought them to the brink of inner
revelation."

But aside from Poe, many of our major literary figures of the
earlier nineteenth century listened (or looked within) and responded to the deep secrets of their minds. Emerson's introspec-
tion was like that of the ordinary "Yankee, . . . consciously
[listening] to his own mind, whose deliberate speech had room for
undertones and further meanings." Thoreau, with his Yankee-
peddler manner of "close and shrewd" reckoning, suggested the
old-time comic Yankee, with his "air of turning the tables on
listeners or observers." Again, "like the legendary Yankee,"

whether with a companion or without, he "seemed always alone." And Rourke fittingly calls attention to Thoreau's allegory of the lost hound, bay horse, and turtledove. Whitman, obviously partaking of both extremes—the "solitary" and the group, is considered by her to have come round "from the generic and inclusive and nationalistic 'I' to the realm of inner feeling"; he uncovered an "inner world" that comedy had already revealed: "reflective rather than emotional." His best poems were soliloquies—for example, his threnody for Lincoln, "When Lilacs Last in the Dooryard Bloomed." Though his "monologue or rhapsody was turned inward," everything flowed out of him; he did not analyze or introspect. But Whitman foreshadowed stream-of-consciousness writing, "the modern mode of inner revelation," with its breaks, shifts, and "final move into . . . soliloquy."

Hawthorne too was concerned with the inner workings of the mind (not necessarily his own), with suppressed emotions—and here Rourke emphasizes *The Scarlet Letter.* Generally Hawthorne's "discoveries" were presented in such a way as to suggest "pure fantasy," and he transformed "regional legends into inner moods." To show the mind's "natural movement," Hawthorne, anticipating a later period of literature, made use of "direct revelation." (Rourke refers to Dimmesdale's feelings, after his woodland encounter with Hester Prynne, and while he moves among the people.)

To exemplify the monologist in the middle distance, between the "solitary" and the member of a group, Rourke takes up the "popular oracle," interacting with his audience to an extent: responding to events of the present and sentiments of the forum, drawing on traditional formulas and modes of expression. She refers fleetingly to the stage Irishman, and Gallagher and Shean of vaudeville fame; and she quotes humorous passages, without citing the authors, from Finley Peter Dunne's turn-of-the-century monologues of the Irish saloonkeeper Mr. Dooley, and from Milt Gross's "Nize Baby" parodies of a Jewish dialect (the "Ferry Tail from de Pite Piper of Hemilton"). Then, after mentioning Will Rogers, the self-styled presidential adviser, and his predecessor of a century earlier, Jack Downing, she refers to the blackface minstrel shows, which, despite the "duologue" of the entertainers, displayed some oracular elements and emphasized the individual actor's monologue. This leads to an important observation on

newspaper-column oracles. Some small-town ones still remained
at the time Rourke was writing *American Humor*, but she says a
bit more about the ones in the cities: monologists, "the sharpest
and most irreverent of social critics"; and she likens the "comic
monologue," as a well-established institution, to the Greek
chorus—the former preserving the traditional custom "of the
complete revelation which tells everything, tells little, and unfolds
the outlines of a character."[17]

The last category of monologist, representing some type of
social group with its own tradition and system of folkways, is
illustrated in the writings of Walt Whitman, Herman Melville,
Edgar Lee Masters, and Sinclair Lewis. Whitman's "generic and
inclusive 'I,'" which to Rourke "has the urgency of many people,"
has already been discussed, in connection with his moving from
that point of reference to the "solitary": what he himself called "a
simple separate person." Regarding Melville, Rourke uses *Moby-
Dick* as a prime example. "Soliloquy, reverie, 'supernatural sur-
misings'" intermix with external events. She makes much of
Ahab's obsession, extending "through the consciousness of" the
Pequod's crew and also—"within the fantastic range of the
narrative—giving shape and color to the natural world." In Ahab's
contest with the whale "the mind [remains] dominant."

By way of placing Edgar Lee Masters's *Spoon River Anthology*,
Rourke first points out that there was antiphony of a sort in Vachel
Lindsay's rhythmic, exuberantly oratorical poems. And antiphony
may be found again in *Spoon River*. The town's inhabitants, and
there is no contradiction here, continue "the monologue, even in
death." As mentioned above in connection with the generic mode
of legend, Masters was less concerned with bringing out the
individual than with the community of Spoon River, "the aggregate type, a way of living." Finally, Sinclair Lewis's characters
appear to have "the unfailing native passion for the monologue:
flood-gates of their talk are opened at a touch." In *Main Street* the
sensory details of daily living are thrown together with such
energy that there is a "sagalike" quality to the movement of life.
Thus Lewis portrays "the generic" and "the human situation"
fades in importance.[18]

By way of summary. I suggested earlier that Rourke was, in
effect, creating another "world out of a wilderness" when she

developed her five representative agents of American humor: the Yankee, the gamecock of the wilderness (backwoodsman *and* riverboatman), the Negro, the stroller (actor *and* revivalist), and the comic poet. To an extent she thought in terms of archetypes, and in the course of her book she would make references to other possible candidates for that good-humor gallery: the Californian, the Babbitt-figure, the "popular oracle." As did William Dean Howells, Rourke responded to "the smiling aspects of life": what she considered "the American character" is a sounding board for various kinds of humorous stimuli—generally nice, socially acceptable ones. For example, humor for vicious degradation, sadistic humor, is not dealt with directly in this book. Rourke does little more than cite the title of George Washington Harris's 1867 collection of antisocial and sadistic tales, *Sut Lovingood*—but she has some cogent remarks in her chapter on the Negro ("That Long-Tail'd Blue") on differing attitudes of whites regarding the Negro as a source of humor.

But underlying all of Rourke's comic stereotypes or archetypes, and generic forms of humor, discussed to an extent in the preceding pages, are certain basic interests: the wonderfully variegated speech of the American people, and the *power* of legend. The book provides a rich sampling of materials representing each, broadly interpreted. Among those falling under the category of American speech forms: the quaint turns of Yankee parlance; rhapsodic poetry; minstrel and vaudeville dialects; John Brougham's musical burlesque of Longfellow, *Pocahontas;* and Ring Lardner's vernacular-monologue stories. Among those under the category of legend: some of Hawthorne's darker tales, Melville's *Moby-Dick,* our bigger-than-life heroes of folklore, Henry James's *The American.*

And underlying such concerns as American speech forms and American legend, is Rourke's quintessential interest: the American tradition as it emanates from the aggregate of the American people. She closes her American humor book on a somewhat familiar note, which underscores this point of view. The American artist needs to be in close contact with native American folk materials, more than he needs the encouragement of his society. It is the job of the critics to discover and make available those folk materials to the artist, who will use them in his own way as he finds "a relationship with the many streams of native character and feeling." Then the individual writer or literary work will not be alone any more, but instead will occupy a place "within a natural sequence."[19]

To boil down the author's argument, by way of an envoy to this chapter: the critic (a researcher and interpreter such as Rourke) makes a world out of the wilderness of the past and the ever-westering American frontier—that is, another world out of the actual world of early-American life. Then the artist-writer takes *that* world and makes his own world from *it*, using the lawless vagaries of his imagination, patterns of tradition (including speech and legend), and a consistent susceptibility to the deep delights of romance. In effect Rourke seems to be strategically extending von Herder's folk-philosophy of art. As indicated, the critic is seen as the necessary intermediary between the folk and the artist or artisan. This means—surely some reader of Rourke must already have noted the significance—that the author of *American Humor*, though no real artist herself, is nevertheless playing a vital role in the *creation* of American art. I will say something more about this matter in my concluding chapter.

CHAPTER 6

Three Likenesses and Some Reflections

IT is necessary now to look briefly at Rourke's remaining books: *Davy Crockett* (1934), *Audubon* (1936), *Charles Sheeler: Artist in the American Tradition* (1938), and the posthumous collection edited by Van Wyck Brooks, *"The Roots of American Culture" and Other Essays* (1942). Each has a place in her developing picture of American cultural life—particularly the last-named work, which represents a small amount of the materials she had prepared for a three-volume *History of American Culture.*

I indicated earlier that her *Trumpets of Jubilee* and *American Humor* are in my view her major works, and I have devoted a good deal of my discussion to her handling of her materials in these two books. As concerns the other four listed above, the fictional biographies of Crockett and Audubon do not stand up alongside her serious works. Pitched to the level of impressionable young children, the books—despite all of the scholarly research that went into their preparation—represent the lay-person side of Rourke's writing. Such commentators as Stanley Edgar Hyman and Kenneth S. Lynn have written them off, in effect, and I shall only make a few selective comments.

I Davy Crockett

As a frontiersman par excellence and folk hero of American tradition and legend, David (Davy) Crockett (1786–1836) would naturally have appealed to Rourke's imagination. Lewis Mumford, in a review of her *Roots of American Culture* essay collection, had this to say about the Crockett and Audubon biographies. They "were fresh efforts to outline the American character at its point of origin, in all its originality. Her own roots reached far back into our pioneer past, through a great-grandfather, George Mayfield, who had been captured as a child by the Indians."[1] Clearly, as Mumford remarked, she loved to collect tall tales, and the book itself is dedicated to two great-aunts—Minerva and Elizabeth Mayfield—"who knew stories about Davy Crockett."

However, her saga of the skillful hunter, backwoods humorist and lawmaker (in the Tennessee legislature and the U.S. Congress), supporter-turned-opponent of Andrew Jackson and the Democratic party, and fallen hero in the Texas War of Independence, emerges as anything but a coherent story. Having read and digested an enormous amount of biographical and historical material on Crockett including the Crockett almanacs—twenty-nine pages are devoted to summarizing the sources—Rourke nevertheless relies heavily on conjectures, on the *perhaps* approach, to develop her overall outline. Moreover, while there are references to the politics of the time—the conflicts of the Jackson Democrats with the Whigs, the dispute with Mexico over the territory of Texas, etc.—the book's overriding concern is with the legends and myths she unearthed, to the glorification of Davy Crockett, hunter and frontier fighter extraordinary. Thus there is little of a serious nature to be gained from this body of Crockett lore. He is of course seen also as another gamecock of the wilderness, boasting (as the role calls for him to do) about being half-horse, half-alligator and doing the traditional superhuman feats. But he is also, and this is the interesting part, seen as being translated into the cosmos. In fact, his death in the fatal Battle of the Alamo, on March 6, 1836, precedes the "Sunshine in His Pocket" chapter. And so the most important event of his life is submerged in a farrago of tall tales about his hunting prowess and his adventures in space, in such a way as to suggest the feats of Popeye, Superman, Captain Marvel, and other pop-culture folk-heroes.

But I believe that *Davy Crockett* may be read on another level, which is important from the standpoint of Rourke's own psychology. In a sense this biography embodies significant features of her own inner life: it involves (as I read it) her identification with two male relatives and her desired membership in the proud group that she felt they represented. The first was her ancestor George Mayfield, stolen by the Creek Indians when he was a baby and raised as one of them. During the War of 1812, Rourke remarks, when General Andrew Jackson was supervising delicate negotiations with the Creeks and the Cherokees, Crockett was serving Jackson as a scout, and "Mayfield, whom Crockett had known in eastern Tennessee, had been chosen to act as Jackson's interpreter"; though Mayfield does not enter directly into the important events of the story, Rourke discusses briefly his life with the Creeks. And, there was another bond "between Crockett and Mayfield besides an acquaintance in that part of Tennessee where both were born." This was "the subtle and many-sided attraction of Indian life."

The second male relative she identified with, in my view, was her own father. Constance Rourke's father, as mentioned earlier, had originally come from southern Ireland; he had died when she was very young; her mother, who never remarried, taught her to cherish his memory. In tracing Davy Crockett's genealogy, near the end of the book, she would speak of a Huguenot forebear, a courtier of Louis XIV, who went to Ireland with his wife, and had a son who married an Irish girl. Their son "married a Huguenot who had come to Ireland, and these two emigrated to Virginia." These were the great-great-grandparents of Davy Crockett. This "Irish family [deriving from the French court] that formed the ancestral line of Davy Crockett" eventually made its way to America's Western frontier;[2] the Irish family represented by Henry Rourke was to find itself in the Western Reserve, where Constance Rourke was born (in Cleveland, Ohio) in 1885. What is suggestive here, and I offer it for what it may be worth, is her profound and worshipful response—like that of a young daughter to a long-departed father—to the bigger-than-life Crockett. She would finally describe this superhero of Irish origin, selecting what suited her best from all the legends, as moving among the heavenly bodies: in fact, restoring the power of motion to the frozen earth and sun.

II   Audubon

What essential meaning did the curious French artist-naturalist, John James Audubon (?–1851), whose life was spent recording the "birds of America," have for Constance Rourke? She tells us, in a note, that Audubon's "biography had its more distant origin in a concern with American frontiers." His writings, however imperfect, "are essential to a knowledge of frontier life along the Ohio and in Louisiana during a significant period, and his development has something to say as to the place of art and science there." Then too, her interest in his character grew; though some of his numerous journals were destroyed by his family, those traditions that had grown up around him seem to have appealed to her, and she also wanted to evoke something of the feel of the nearly vanished wilderness within which he worked.[3]

Something else emerges from her story of Audubon's stormy career, with its financial and professional reverses, family migrations, prolonged absences from home, upsurges of humor, and the eventual publication of *Birds of America* and the *Ornithological Biography*. This element is giantism, or to put it another way, the epic scale, and it relates somehow to at least two familiar Rourkean topics: tradition and legend. Through much of her writing she would return periodically to the mystique of hugeness, as though responding to some deep inner need for a fulfilling self-satisfaction.

Rourke sees in Audubon's fragmentary records of his labors in the American wilderness, during the first half of the nineteenth century, a "panorama . . . in the epical scale, achieved early in a period when the spirit of the epic was beginning to" develop here "in cycles of legends about the frontier, already centering upon such characters as Boone and Crockett," culminating (from a literary standpoint) "two decades later in the work of Whitman and Melville and lesser others." She regards Audubon's method, like that of Whitman, as "largely personal"; within it he conveyed "an immense zest." Audubon was able to live "in the broad natural world" and to enjoy his "five senses to the full." As for Audubon's painting, "the epical scope appeared fully" there; he was possessed of "flowing, uncalculating abundance" and would always be stimulated by "Magnitude in an undertaking." Again, "Magnitudes were there to which he felt akin, not least in humor."[4] Rourke's attempt to "place" Audubon may have a special significance, given her own confusion of styles and aims (regarding excessive size, for example), and her limited acceptance by academics and critics. Audubon, she points out, "was as far removed from the artists of the studios in Philadelphia, New York, London, and Paris as he was from the museum naturalists."[5]

Rourke, as her book makes evident, wants her readers to be aware of the distinctive Audubon design, the hallmark of the illustrations in *Birds of America* that elevated the huge book beyond the reach of the works of less talented men such as Alexander Wilson, "the first American ornithologist." We may appreciate this design as an outgrowth of Audubon's large, abundant, epical scale. At the same time Rourke does not neglect such important matters as Audubon's essential preference for a mixture of water colors and pastels, over oils—which he was not comfortable with; and she touches on related matters such as the aquatint and engraving processes that made his illustrations of birds and nature scenes reproducible by the printer.

Early in the 1820s, when Audubon was still relatively unknown, his excellent representations of birds were slow to receive proper recognition, because there did not yet exist any "standard by which to gauge them." Yet, apparently without imitating earlier models of flower and bird painting, Audubon had approached original American forms. (The former were the paintings of Flemish and French artists of early modern times, of the Pennsylvania Germans who had once been Audubon's neighbors, and of "the Indian decoration with which he was familiar.") But there was this distinction. While they all made use of "abstract forms," Audubon "used naturalism in pure design." Regarding what actually lay behind his figures, in pictorial terms, Rourke speaks of "his almost habitual lack of concern with backgrounds."

Even when he came out of obscurity and gained a measure of fame, Audubon encountered the opposition of the critics, who did not recognize "the constant pressure of his sense of design." One particularly nasty attacker was John Neal, a hack-fiction writer and editor. Rourke answers his accusations (among other things, Neal attributed a good bit of the art work to other hands than Audubon's) by invoking that basic concept. "Design marches through all of Audubon's work; in study after study his instinctive preoccupation is clear." In his work there is "an even flow of pattern; the originals [reveal] no break in technique or handling." Neither a romantic nor a philosopher, this "'American woodsman'" who had as a youngster studied under the French artist Jacques David possessed a visual "sense of order and design."[6]

If there is more to Rourke's interest in this multifaceted man around whom so many traditions have developed, than his character and the epic scale of his endeavors, I suggest it may be the following. Audubon was worth identifying with for reasons that might carry weight with a chronicler of artists and their work, like Constance Rourke, inclined to romanticize the biographical subject almost out of reality. These reasons relate to one of the most psychologically bracing verses in the Bible, Psalms 118:22 (and repeated in Matthew, Mark, Luke, and Acts): "The stone which the builders refused is become the head stone of the corner." Rourke devotes a good deal of effort, particularly at the end of the book, to advance the tenuous notion that the obscurely-born and reputedly-illegitimate John James Audubon might actually have been the Lost Dauphin of France: the hitherto-unidentified son of Marie Antoinette and Louis XVI. Not only did Audubon's humble, obscure birth suggest to Rourke's romantic imagination the very opposite, in the way of origins, but his lifelong struggle against poverty, failure, and mistreatment by the critics was rewarded by the immortality of rich, persistent legend. How heartwarming to a gifted but insufficiently appreciated craftsperson in her own right (Rourke, for example), to retell a great American saga in which the last finally does come first, or wherein the lowly is ultimately brought very high.

III   Charles Sheeler

Constance Rourke's "informal biography" of the American artist and photographer Charles Sheeler (1883–1965), up to about 1938, made extensive use of his professional notes and of conversations she had held with him. The volume is shorter than her earlier books and vastly different from them in style and approach, if not in ultimate aim. Lavishly illustrated with black-and-white reproductions of Sheeler's most important works, the work provides a fascinating commentary on art movements of the earlier twentieth century.

Charles Sheeler is something of a polemic, rather a plea—for us to take an interest in our early traditions (in art for example) so that we can preserve our continuity as a cultural entity and advance to greater heights. Rourke must refute the stinging argument of Van Wyck Brooks (who is cited directly and indirectly here) that "our civilization . . . had failed to produce a culture in which the arts could flourish or an audience that was responsive," as a result of which "the artist had frequently been driven abroad, or if he remained at home he had led a thwarted existence." Moreover, there was a related argument to attack: "all our art was necessarily an offshoot of European art."

Rourke would use several distinct lines of defense to argue that we had a nourishing American culture, with traditional native forms of expression, for the artist. The first line was *confession and avoidance*. Sheeler, early in his career, did experience the "isolation of the American artist [that] was Brooks's theme"; not having the kind of guidance that would have been helpful, he chose as his teacher William M. Chase, "whose ideas were radically at variance with his own latent power." At this time styles and philosophies in the world of art were in a state of flux, but "something resembling a movement, if not a school, had developed in which both artists and writers were loosely joined."

The second line was *refutation from the evidence*. A "precisionist" of line and of geometric form carried almost to the point of abstraction, a laureate of the architectural scene—Sheeler was not working within the mainstream of contemporary art (though he "had struck back to our primary sources in dimensional form"). And, "according to a formula which even then was in vogue, the American artist who chose a more difficult mode should have been experiencing a profound isolation." However, Sheeler's work was well accepted by the public at this period: the third decade. Possibly, Rourke suggests, this was because he "was working in the American grain, not against it."

The third line was *direct testimony by the principal*. Speaking of Chartres Cathedral, which he admired intensely and had photographed a number of times, Sheeler acknowledged that the ethnic tradition and background underlying it were elements in which he had no part. "'It seems to be a persistent necessity for me to feel a sense of derivation from the country in which I live and work.'"[7]

To present Sheeler's contributions to American art, Rourke discusses his use of understatement, his self-effacement as an artist, his use of light in rendering design. She compares Sheeler with the classic artists because of his stressing "the way in which the subject has been perceived" over the subject itself. Among the book's four dozen or so reproductions of paintings, drawings, and photographs, some of Sheeler's more striking linear studies include: *Church Street El, Self-Portrait* (a telephone in front of a windowpane), *View of New York* (a partly opened window in a studio), *The Open Door, Upper Deck, American Landscape*, and *Classic Landscape* (the last two showing railroad yards and tall

smokestacks in an industrial area). At variance with the naturalism and impressionism of his time, he sought "the underlying
order" in his subject.

Surveying Sheeler's career from her tradition-oriented perspective, Rourke would be able to go into such matters as form and
design in art, and classicism versus romanticism. In architecture,
Sheeler "had discovered forms that were basic in American
creative experience"; these were "source-forms." To him, "Design"
seemed "a latent order which he [had] revealed rather than
something . . . superimposed." He said of his painting that he
"'had a continued interest in natural forms and . . . sought the best
use of them for the enhancement of design.'" His "search for form
in American sources would be enough to give his work a unique
position even if there were nothing more to say of it." Speaking of
the early settlers' barns in Bucks County, Pennsylvania, he felt that
their shapes "were determined by function"; the individual's "final
satisfaction," in Sheeler's opinion, came from the firm "relationship between the parts." And he concluded (as a Gestalt psycholo-
gist might have done) that this could well matter "to the artist who
considers the working of the parts toward the consummation of
the whole as of primary importance in a picture."

In her handling of another important topic, classicism versus
romanticism, Rourke extends the range of her treatment of
Sheeler's work as it relates to modern art. Referring to America's
"classic revival" of Greco-Roman architecture when our country
was young, she mentions the then-current idea "that we were to
emulate the Golden Age in our rising civilization." However, in
her view "the classic revival represented one of our thoroughly
romantic aspirations." It is her argument that we have traditionally been followers of romanticism, not classicism. She suggests
that "we have never had a classic art" here and "that we *were* the
romantic movement during the nineteenth century and even
earlier"; life on the frontier, the most typically American "phases
of the national character," reflected romanticism's "stresses and
strains." But Rourke attempts to demonstrate that Sheeler, having
"made himself a pathfinder in the use of American traditions in
art," his accomplishment being "the more striking since it was a
solitary venture," was rather a classicist than a romantic.

Her line of reasoning is interesting to follow, not only because it
goes back to her essential views on conserving our early American

traditions in the arts and crafts—and to this extent Rourke's position reflects classicism—but because of its intricate philosophical analysis. Briefly stated, and with a caveat regarding oversimplification, it is this. Romanticism favors the expression of emotion, classicism restrains it. In romanticism, which is bent on discovery, "change is a touchstone"; if the past is called up the artist looks upon it "not . . . with serenity but with nostalgia." Classicism, on the other hand, takes what "has been discovered; it is rooted in tradition." Now right at this point Rourke provides the transition that will enable her to explain Sheeler as a classicist.

Although classicism has its roots in tradition, "if it is a living force its accepted inheritance will be freshly transformed." Sheeler, in his work with, for example, "architectural forms in Bucks County" (the halftone reproduction of the starkly elemental *Bucks County Barn* gives an idea of what he was about) and handicrafts in that area, "was tapping main sources." He was drawing on cultural expressions which conveyed the serene character of communal life, of close similarities in origin, custom, and belief—which Rourke associates with the frontier settlements.

How did Sheeler, by "tapping main sources," transform the legacy of tradition to make classicism "a living force" in his art? An opponent of naturalism in art (with "its implications as to the unorderly, . . . swift impressionism, . . . [and] illusion versus permanences"), Sheeler stood for "a full dedication to the subject and a search for the underlying order to which it belonged." Contrary to the approach of the romantics and to what his teacher, Chase, had urged, he played down his own individuality in his art. His concern was not with the self-touting bravura of the artist, not even with the subject per se (no contradiction here, with the above remark about his dedication to his subject). Rather, his concern was with the way that the subject was perceived, and this involved for the highly individualistic and nonconformist Sheeler, overall form. Thus his individual works exemplify a classic unity, "a singleness of order," which "is the essence of the classic approach."[8]

In the course of her absorbing survey of Sheeler's career up to 1938, Rourke also touches on a number of other interesting items: his Welsh and Irish background (which matched her own), his sense of humor, and the theatrical spirit that has always been part of the American character. All told, *Charles Sheeler*—really a

collaborative venture between biographer and subject—is a genu-
inely satisfying book about a good artist, too easily forgotten by a
later generation.

IV   The Roots of American Culture

A year or so after Constance Rourke died, Van Wyck Brooks,
whose thesis of "the American artist pitifully languishing on
barren native soil" she was bent on refuting, edited a collection of
her essays. Two had already appeared in print: "American Art: A
Possible Future," in the July 1935 issue of *Magazine of Art;* and
"Voltaire Combe," in the October 7, 1939, issue of the *Nation.* The
long title-essay, which serves as the book's underpinning, opens the
collection. It is followed by the longest of all, a 101-page treatise
on "The Rise of Theatricals"; this is broken up into six parts: "The
Indian Background," "Susannah Rowson," "After the Revolution,"
"New England," "The West," and "The Elder Booth." The next,
fittingly, is on "Early American Music"; the remaining essays are
"The Shakers," "A Note on Folklore," "Voltaire Combe," "Traditions for a Negro Literature," and "American Art: A Possible
Future."

Considering Rourke's differences with Brooks over the position
of the American artist, writer or otherwise, on native ground—for
example, her *Charles Sheeler* attacks Brooks's argument quite
effectively—his editing some of her papers on that subject is
curious. He speaks of her projected masterwork, the three-volume
History of American Culture, and praises the "charming qualities
of style and . . . freshness of feeling" of her "exceptionally
interesting" earlier books. Only retrospectively could a reader "see
how fully they were outgrowths of a single conception and a
governing idea," the idea that was to have been uncovered in her
History of American Culture and that gives her endeavors their
importance. Brooks conveys the intensity with which Rourke,
deeply rooted in our Middle West, considered that notion of our
having "failed to produce a culture in which the arts could
flourish." Quite ominous if true, because "no art had ever reached
a point where it could speak a world-language without an
inheritance of local expression behind it." She knew well that if she
could show that we had this native esthetic tradition, "the
consequences might be important for American art."

Brooks mentions her having been attracted to the ideas of the nineteenth-century German critic-philosopher Johann Gottfried von Herder, and provides a brief summary. The roots of a given culture lie within its "folk-forms" and "folk-arts"; the "folk-forms" are of the essence "of the communal experience and expression"; "the fine arts [spring] out of the folk-arts"; etc. At the same time Rourke was dealing with the entrenched belief that we had no folk art or folk expression of our own—other than what was carried over from Europe; thus, until enough European culture was imported here, we would continue to suffer from a "'culture lag.'" By no means did Rourke want us to be cut off from "main streams of European culture," Brooks points out; what she wanted was for us to find "our own center." Did we actually have "a long folk-life behind us" with "creative forces" constituting "an esthetic tradition?"

Which brings him to Rourke's ongoing purpose. She wished to show that such a tradition existed, and to make this evident by various means. This tradition, if she were able to collect sufficient materials, "would declare itself through them"; she wished to allow future Americans to gain access to "our natural inheritance" so that they might be nourished through "characteristic native forms" which would serve "as points of departure." Rourke's "work was thus mainly exploratory, and she threw herself into it with a zest that took her into every corner of the country." Rourke's was not an antiquarian interest; "she never lost sight of her purpose in studying" the folk arts. Now Brooks, utterly abandoning his essential creed (which was so much at variance with hers), admits that she had brought together "proofs of a rich creative life in our past," finding therein signs "of distinctive native American elements." Though "our early culture" may have had European origins, it "diverged from Europe in accordance with our native experience and needs." Praising her work lavishly, deeply regretting that she could not complete her "very ambitious task," which was to have included every "phase of American culture," Brooks mentions that he could save but a small number of scraps out of the large body of her partly written papers.[9]

Why then Brooks included two already published essays is unclear. He has erred, I strongly feel, in putting together this fragmentary cultural history, for it weakens somewhat Rourke's essential argument and highlights the shortcomings in her approach to her subject. He did her a disservice by publishing her poorly worked-out ideas and flimsy reasonings. There is, however, considerable merit in the long analytical piece, "The Rise of Theatricals," although in view of all the culture barriers, her argument that Indian treaties were our first dramas seems misleading. "Early American Music" and "The Shakers" are generally informative and well-presented. The illustrative fable of an almost unknown nineteenth-century painter—S.E. Hyman apparently took "Voltaire Combe" as fact, as did *Time's* book reviewer (August 10, 1942)—is interesting for what it says about American life and art from the early 1800s to the early 1900s. But in my view there are certain things seriously wrong with the book as a whole.

First, an air of unreality floats over the work, largely because of Rourke's steady insistence that the American artist needs to work out of a body of communal tradition. Endless reiterations and vast generalizations on this matter fill the book; many of them occur in the very weak essays, "The Roots of American Culture" and "American Art: A Possible Future." There is altogether too much begging of the question throughout. Rourke seems wishfully unrealistic in seeing cultural archaeologists like herself as playing a vital role in the careers of American artists, supplying them with necessary raw materials taken from a common body of folkways. Thus: "A sensitive historical criticism would seem a major necessity [for these artists], broadly grounded in native research as well as in esthetics. A prodigious amount of work is still to be done in the way of unearthing, defining, and synthesizing our traditions, and finally in making them known through simple and natural means." But—most artists do not work in so history-conscious and programmatic a way.

Then there are glaring omissions in her consideration of art forms emerging from communal tradition. For instance, not nearly enough is made of popular music, "white" forms or "black" forms, since colonial times for the former and the nineteenth-century minstrel shows (and the much earlier juba-dancing of plantation slaves) for the latter. Nothing is said of famous magazine illustrators, whose elegant covers, posters, and pictorial sketches influenced American popular taste from the earlier nineteenth century onward. And what of the numerous popular-art media—children's literature, comics, radio, cinema, graphic layouts for advertising—with interesting roots in old-time tradition? True, these essays, mere bits and pieces of Rourke's proposed *History,* do not pretend to provide thorough coverage. Yet Rourke seems largely unaware of the complex variety of expressions of popular art and thought that have long been available to us. And, so much space in the book is devoted to repeating the same simple notion to such modest purpose, that additional substantive materials would have been welcome.

Another shortcoming involves semantic confusions and blurrings. I have not found in Rourke's work an adequate distinction between popular-art forms and fine art. I have never felt that she worked from a set of standards that specified the rigid requirements of the latter, as opposed to relaxed guidelines for the former. Her *Charles Sheeler* and portions of her other writings do show an awareness of the techniques of the fine, or high, artist, but my point is that in the essay collection assembled by Van Wyck Brooks some such distinction and set of standards would have been most helpful. Rourke does admit that possibly the pioneer's "folk-handicrafts" have been overvalued, though she acknowledges their "lasting creative values" and what they reveal "of visual and tactile skills." Yet she will simply go on to say that "the typical pioneer or frontiersman was master of those daily and primitive arts that have often afforded an ancestry for the fine arts." There are one or two other brief hints along the same line, but nothing of a substantive nature.

This is in "American Art: A Possible Future." In "The Roots of American Culture," she traces the philosophy of "the popular or folk-arts" from Montaigne to Herder and carries it practically to her own time. To near-contemporary observers whatever "is quaint or exaggerated is folk" and "possible relationships of the folk-arts to the fine arts [have not] seemed basic." Attempting here to explain the development of "dominant forms of expression" in the life of the folk—they result primarily from "popular acceptances"—she says little about the determinants of a group's art forms, save those stemming from religion or superstition. A similar superficiality is seen in her vague comments and misleading bias regarding art forms of the folk, as opposed to "peaks of achievement," masterpieces, such definitive indexes of cultural quality as the fine arts and genius, and the widespread notion that the arts are luxuries.

Lastly, there are a number of errors and the like, which Brooks should have caught. For example, Rourke would make very much of the Gestalt concept of the dynamic configuration, as applied to culture. She obtained this view from Ruth Benedict, quotes her on the subject, quotes another famous anthropologist (Robert H. Lowie) in a similar connection, and refers a number of times to this important idea, without using the word "Gestalt." Things all hang together in a culture as elsewhere, is the idea here; one component cannot be removed from the dynamic whole and considered in isolation. Yet, when speaking of the work of the American painter Charles E. Burchfield, she will apparently overlook all she has said about the configurational (Gestalt) view of things, and in fact all she has said about the shaping forces of the American character, to make this strange generalization. "If, as has been said, his deserted mansions stand aloof from the earth on which they are planted, this separation from environment has been a large part of our experience."

On another matter, Rourke, being very interested in the abstract (in art and thought), a mode she handles very shakily, comments that in the seventeenth and eighteenth centuries, "Puritan and non-Puritan alike were influenced . . . by the tendency toward the abstract in Calvinistic theology, and equally by the general turn toward abstraction which came in England with the Reformation and took many speculative forms." This baffler, which is followed by the amazing judgment that "the journeyman builder" (whether or not he was a Puritan) obtained from "abstract values . . . an undefined pleasure" and "even took a sensuous delight in the elimination of ornamental detail," occurs in "American Art: A Possible Future." In the title essay of the book, Rourke sees the Reformation as having had seemingly self-contradictory effects: it gave "dignity to the common man," while at the same time being influential "in detaching art from the ruck of common life." This resulted in the individual's being "given sole responsibility for his eternal fate." To take up only this last point, Rourke had spent a great deal of effort in *Trumpets of Jubilee* pointing out that many people after the Reformation—those under the influence of Calvinist-predestination theology, for example—were psychologically afflicted because they felt they were given no responsibility for their eternal fate.

But Rourke also sees the Reformation, especially through the medium of Calvinism, as having had this effect on the individual: "he was cast into a complex and bewildering inner sphere, that of analytical self-scrutiny." And this kind of probing of the self, she has no doubt, "would have developed if Luther and Calvin had never lived." She entertains the view ("it may even be argued," is the way she puts it) "that the Reformation arose because of an inevitable drift of the exploratory human spirit toward inner complexities rather than that the Reformation created them." Possibly the most amazing feature of this sweeping away of fact and logic here is this. Shapers of human destiny (for good or ill), "representative men," are not really taken into account. Historical changes, like the production of much of our art, seem to derive from the masses. Though Rourke does say, a little further along in this essay, that she is not exalting "the common arts or common themes over the luxury arts," it is hard to escape the conclusion that her stress is generally on what comes from the people at large. What might at first glance be taken as exceptions to this will be commented on in the concluding chapter of this biography.

Some more startling remarks might be mentioned. In her extended discussion ("The Roots of American Culture") of important colonial towns such as Salem, Massachusetts, and Annapolis, Maryland, Rourke has a good deal of interest to say about the general layout, the architecture, and the pictorial art. She describes a painting "of a lovely Annapolis lady with a volume of Locke on her lap," which "suggests ideas that had a far-reaching influence upon the philosophy of the Revolution"; it "reveals a typical concern of the ladies of Annapolis." This cultural thesis predicated on the portrait of a lady becomes an introduction to what reads like one more insubstantial line of reasoning. "If the ladies were as noted for their interest in intellectual matters, they were also famous for their devotion to fashion and gay apparel," etc. Which leads to a brief discussion of "a quaint and ancient custom [preserved] from the medieval courts. The gentlemen tilted for ladies' favors on horseback with lances and rings. Even now in Maryland this custom survives." No source for this information is cited, nor is it made clear how this is relevant to a tracing of our cultural roots.

Speaking, in "The Shakers," of two separate domestic altercations in the earlier 1800s over Shaker membership of one party only—quarrels rich in spicy details, provocatively described in a body of "controversial [pamphlet] literature"—Rourke generalizes as follows. "When such tales of real life were publicly available the novel perhaps lacked a function." Finally (again in "American Art: A Possible Future"), she comments, straightface, on what might be done to decorate more of the "empty . . . walls of our many gathering-places" with murals. "An acute sense of the more conspicuous phases of social expression among us, as in revivals, camp-meetings, political demonstrations, lodges, parades, and even lynching [*sic*], might give the American muralist a knowledge of basic social outlines as well as an extended range of materials."[10]

The Roots of American Culture, I feel, is an extremely uneven work, in a way that none of Rourke's other books is, not even *Troupers of the Gold Coast* or *Davy Crockett*. Whatever her projected three-volume work on the *History of American Culture* would have been like, at least in one very important sense, this *Roots of American Culture* essay-volume is not entirely of her own doing.

CHAPTER 7

Finale and Encore

CONSTANCE Rourke emerges from her sizable body of cultural studies of American art and American life, from her placid, semiretired existence in Grand Rapids with her aging and overly demanding mother in an unusually close relationship—as a striking example of one of the typical figures she has made so much of in *American Humor*: the comic poet. A great deal is involved in my calling *her* an American comic poet. There was her quick, lyrical responsiveness to geographic regions and to the kinds of settlers (English, Scotch, Irish, European) who migrated there. Then, her straining imagination, which sensed fantasy and rhapsody in so many places that would leave others cold: an imagination at once responsive to giants, to the lure of legend, to the mystery of the all-promising theatrical stage; an imagination that enabled her to create her own (better-than-actual) world out of the wilderness of historical and familial tradition. And, there was her profound and joyous attachment to the people at large. Fittingly, given her predilections, she would title an important chapter in *American Humor*, which devotes considerable space to Walt Whitman and his poetry, "I Hear America Singing." But the poet in the popular view has long been taken as an impractical, unrealistic individual whose thoughts run helter-skelter. And even in this regard, discounting slightly for interpretive bias, I feel that Rourke fits the broad description of comic poet.[1]

Before discussing Rourke's significance as a writer, and her contribution to literature (essentially, American literature), I wish to quote briefly a number of commentators and critics—pro and con—who over the decades have given conventional views of the lady's work: taking her literally, possibly too literally. My appearing to have done so myself, in the body of this book up to the

concluding chapter, must be understood in terms of the need to
examine her important writings empirically prior to making any
final judgments. As to the statements to be quoted here, I shall not
divide them into partisan categories. Rather, since Rourke is well-
known for *American Humor* but has not aroused very much
critical controversy over the last half-century or so, I shall take
them up in chronological order.

Lewis Mumford, writing appreciatively of *The Roots of American Culture* and of Rourke's cultural-historical investigations (in
the *Saturday Review of Literature* in August of 1942) stated that
"hers was one of the great names of our generation." Rourke "was
equally at home in music, literature, painting, drama, and the
crafts"; nothing was beyond her, and "she had what few ordinary
field workers [in the cultural history of this country] have: a sense
of relative values . . . all her special items gained value by their
relevance to the greater whole she carried in her mind."[2]

A minor and very brief dispute of sorts, at about this time, did
grow out of another review of *The Roots of American Culture*.
Alfred Kazin, in a generally favorable essay in the *New Republic*,
made a number of cogent points but spoke candidly about
Rourke's limitations. He stressed what she had sought in her work:
"'the irreducible [i.e., native] element'" that was at the core of a
national character—"what so many modern Americans have lost,
what so many Europeans have established as the first principle of
a human existence—the sense of locality, the simple happiness of
belonging to a particular culture." Yet Constance Rourke "failed
us" in not doing more than trying "to locate and define a native
inheritance"; having reestablished what often had not even been
"known, she took it for granted . . . that the way ahead was in
some sense clear; that we had as definable a future as we had
available a tradition." Creative though she was, when dealing
with folklore, Rourke "confused the pleasure she took in her own
explorations, even the subtle grace she conferred upon them in all
her books, with an imminent opportunity in art for others." Stated
somewhat differently, her failure lay in the fact that she did not
draw "the wealth of patterns and skills she had uncovered into *our*
'natural sequence' now, our contemporary predicament and
need." If all the individual elements Rourke picked out—
distinctive furniture, folk-hero legends, old-time music, etc.,
etc.—"speak to us, what is to be learned from them?" Having
what Rourke called "'the irreducible element'" is not enough:

Americans will "never know what it is" until they are able to "use it without piety or the endless frightened supplications to the past. Commemoration, somehow, is never enough."[3]

A burning rejoinder to Kazin's review-and-evaluation article soon appeared in the *Nation*. It was written by Margaret Marshall, a journalist and close friend of Constance Rourke, who had written a heartfelt tribute to her, also in the *Nation* ("Constance Rourke: Artist and Citizen") shortly after her death the year before. Incensed that Kazin, alone among the five reviewers of *The Roots of American Culture* that she read, failed to give Rourke's work uncritical support, would in fact qualify any kind of praise for Rourke's achievement, Marshall suggested that some kind of pitched battle was being waged by opposing critical camps, with Constance Rourke the victim. She "has become enmeshed in a critical quarrel which is today particularly sharp." From the standpoint of the 1980s it would seem that Marshall was exaggerating here, by creating a picture of a fierce factional struggle; however, a few explanatory details may be of use.

These were the two warring groups (of "critical lions"), according to Marshall: those "who have appreciated" Rourke's investigative endeavors, and the ones "who have never, publicly at least, deigned to taste her wares"; and Marshall suspected that the latter faction was strengthened in its prejudice against Rourke's writings by "the very identity of" the former faction. Quite fairly—possibly even self-critically—Marshall regretted the tendency of "Rourke's admirers . . . to diminish her stature by seizing upon those elements which nourish their own particular interests." Now the former faction included the "pro-Americans," exalting what Marshall called "the home town": in the form of Van Wyck Brooks's "genteel New England," or of "the 'wholesome' anti-intellectual hinterland." The latter included "the avant-garde," who advocated "the international point of view"; Marshall saw these as having Europe on the brain, so to speak—rejecting what they called "the chauvinistic school," frightened of displaying too much interest in the American people or folk. Paradoxically, Marshall continued, this group was "often far to the left in politics and . . . therefore committed to a belief in 'the people.'" What might have turned into an embarrassingly acrimonious debate between self-styled loyalists and socialists (or communist sympathizers), in the latter part of 1942 and thereafter, seems however to have soon dissipated. Thus the Marshall-Kazin exchange—

which will still concern us momentarily—was reduced to a tempest in a teapot.

The central point of disagreement, the crux of the little dispute between Marshall and Kazin, with neither willing to make fundamental concessions, bears on the lasting value of Rourke's work; for that reason I shall restate it. Did she, gathering and describing the remnants and relics of traditional American art forms in so many different media, give contemporary artists, artisans, craftsmen what they could actually use to develop their "craft or sullen art"? Marshall's steadfast assertion—and it is strange that she and Kazin could use the same language, at the same period of time, about the same documentary materials with reference to the same concerns, and come to diametrically opposing conclusions—was that Rourke certainly did. "She not only proclaimed her critical objective, over and over again, to be a synthesis that would be relevant to our 'contemporary predicament.' She actually accomplished it, on the limited scale of a single volume, in 'American Humor.'"[4]

What could Kazin say? Replying in an early issue of the *Nation*, he tried to explain his position again, incidentally praising *American Humor* as "one of the prime works on the American imagination." Skilled though Rourke was in analyzing her findings, Kazin argued, she "could only examine fragments of [her recovered] materials in modern and contemporary writers." Rourke failed to "approach criticism on its contemporary ground; she thought she did, and Miss Marshall takes the will for the deed." And Kazin went on to criticize *American Humor's* later chapters (perhaps he was a little bit inconsistent) and the last chapter of *The Roots of American Culture* ("American Art: A Possible Future") for their "essential vagueness . . . that is inevitable in view of her concentration on [and "her joyful recovery of"] our pre-industrial culture," and her fulfilled desire to demonstrate that Americans had their own fine native culture.

What was Marshall's next move? By way of rejoinder to this reply, she made it clear that she did not care for Kazin's (supposed) dismissal of Rourke, and reiterated her essential belief about the utility value of what the latter produced. Rourke gave "us a fresh discovering view of the sources that James and Dickinson and Whitman and Poe drew upon . . . [and] by so doing she made the reader aware of the sources of his own thought and feeling. Is that criticism or commemoration?"[5]

The anonymous writer of the entry on Rourke in *The National Cyclopaedia of American Biography* (1945) gave a generally favorable overview of her work, while mentioning some criticism, apparently from what Marshall called the "avant-garde." Thus, she was one of "that group of historians who interpret history from an anthropological and social rather than the conventional approach"; her contention was that cultural growth did not represent a process distinct "from the development of the people of a country," rather it was "a spontaneous artistic activity" maintained side by side "with the growth of civilization and government." Although "Critics of her writings have pointed out that she minimized foreign influence in describing the development of America's fine arts . . . her lively, witty picture of America's cultural heritage was everywhere acclaimed and the value recognized of" her quite extensive discoveries "concerning persons and activities too small for the conventional historian to notice."[6]

One of the few real "boosts" Rourke was to receive in the realm of American scholarship was her recognition as a major critic by Stanley Edgar Hyman, in his important survey of critical movements (not necessarily with a body of followers): *The Armed Vision: A Study in the Methods of Modern Literary Criticism* (first published in 1948). Though Hyman attacked a number of his twelve subjects (Van Wyck Brooks, T. S. Eliot, Edmund Wilson, for example) and grandly pointed out the shortcomings and vulnerabilities of the members of his pantheon, on balance his treatment of Rourke was quite generous. Deeply interested in serious folklore investigation, mythography, cultural anthropology, Hyman devoted some of his chapter on "Constance Rourke *and Folk Criticism*" to the nineteenth-century English anthropological school (according to him, Rourke was hardly aware of it) and to other elements in the folk-criticism movement. A few of his remarks are worth notice.

Regarding Rourke's efforts in trying to gather a body of folk-art materials and traditions for use by later creative workers in the arts, Hyman took her work to be "both analytic and synthetic"; this combination of modes, he felt, made for "one of the most promising activities in American criticism, unfortunately carried on since her death by no one." Though Rourke "was always on the verge of relating her American material to the great stream of world folk culture," she did not have "the background, the learning, perhaps the imagination," for the accomplishment of that task. And so she restricted her aim to the creation of "a specifically American and democratic folk tradition" which would counter "the sophisticated and undemocratic European formal tradition defined by men like Eliot." By way of conclusion, Hyman paid tribute to Rourke for doing even more than analyzing and synthesizing folk-art materials for future artists. She also educated "provincial critics like Van Wyck Brooks," and popularized little-known and misunderstood "figures and cultural phenomena" from the past; again there is mention of Voltaire Combe, with Hyman (as I said earlier) taking Rourke's hypothetical village-artist as a real person. Hyman considered her to have been "a democrat and a patriot" in a genuine and honorable sense, and felt that if she had lived longer, "she would have helped the American folk and the individual artists it has" produced to take "their places in the cultural history of the world."[7]

Another "boost" for Rourke, though not as significant as Hyman's, was given by the American literature scholar Kenneth S. Lynn, editor of *The Comic Tradition in America* (1958), one of the significant anthologies of American humor. In 1963 Lynn brought out a Harcourt, Brace & World paperback edition of Rourke's first book, *Trumpets of Jubilee*. To this he added an informative introduction dealing at length with important literary currents, critics, and works of the 1910s and 1920s—his aim being to provide a cultural and historical background that would help explain what Rourke was trying to do in *Trumpets*. There is an interesting and complicated double-perspective in that work, and it is stimulating to consider Lynn's description of the rage, among our important writers, for what was new, really new—not long before Rourke produced her book—in the light of Rourke's keynote stress on the apocalyptic urge of Lyman Beecher to *make all things new*.

As Lynn saw it, Constance Rourke's "unique achievement" in her "first book is that she alone, among all the members of her generation who were bent on exploring the cultural resources of the country, was willing to honor the spokesmen of an older America for their own sake as well as for the sake of present and future American artists." No "pious antiquarian . . . [or] debunker or . . . myth-maker," the "sympathetic and objective" Rourke was rather "a superb cultural historian," whose "quiet but compelling example" has enabled her to exert "a continuing influence on writers concerned with the American past for more than thirty-five years."[8]

Some years later, in a short biographical sketch of Constance Rourke for *Notable American Women*, Lynn modified his judgment of *Trumpets*. (He also identified her father as a lawyer, as other encyclopedia sources on Rourke have done—but I find this entirely at variance with personal accounts of those who knew the family.) Though praising "the astute literary analysis of *Uncle Tom's Cabin*" and Rourke's "suggestive comparison" of Stowe's talent with that of Hawthorne, he felt that "the book today seems disappointingly superficial." The author's "key failure is her reduction of Lyman Beecher's religion to a caricature that might have been composed by H. L. Mencken." Whether or not Lynn was too hard on Rourke at this point is difficult to say: I have indicated earlier that the biblical and theological background of the "make all things new" revivalists, reformers, and utopians was not covered properly in *Trumpets*. But Lynn reserves warm praise for *American Humor*. "To her prodigious scholarship" Rourke brought "a matured style with all the pictorial qualities of her earlier prose but more precise and judicious, capable of registering the sadness that lies at the base of American humor as well as of delighting in the comic extravagances of the national spirit."[9]

Marie Caskey, in an article in the *Dictionary of National Biography* (1973), made a number of interesting observations, some of which are worth mentioning here. Regarding *Trumpets of Jubilee:* "With an uncertain grasp of religious history, she could produce only a superficial analysis of New England theology in the thought of Lyman Beecher . . ., or even in the broader life of his children. The whole book, in fact, is marred by a dwelling on the brash and bizarre." *American Humor* "is still fresh and significant." The author's "racy, zestful style made *American Humor* a classic of historical portraiture." *Charles Sheeler* was Rourke's "most fully realized critical study." By way of summary: despite "the liveliness of her writing and the suggestive hints her studies contain, today's reader notices in her work as a whole her failure to appreciate fully the uses of the comparative approach and her tendency to celebrate folk tradition and popular culture at the expense of analysis and generalization." Though Rourke possessed "a perceptive yet modest critical apparatus, she left even her best studies" unfinished, "and ultimately they have limited explanatory power." But these "were the shortcomings of a pioneer who" strongly stimulated "the field of American literary history."[10]

Finally, there is the Yale doctoral dissertation in modern history, *A World Out of a Wilderness: Constance Rourke and the Search for a Usable Past* (1974), by Joan Shelley Rubin, and its adaptation as a book, *Constance Rourke and American Culture* (1980). An analysis of Rourke's efforts as a critic, vis-ˢᴹa-vis the critical labors of such eminent figures as Brooks, Parrington, DeVoto, Mumford, Matthiessen, et al., Rubin's work contains some particularly cogent observations, pro and con, regarding Rourke's accomplishments. Rubin saw her as a myth-maker, because she was so impressionable and because of her imprecise speech: "'seems,'" "'as if,'" "'as though.'" Aside from her "tentative language," Rourke tried "to establish American traditions," not just record them; this involved giving "traditional characteristics" to almost "every movement in American thought" that she treated. Rubin felt that possibly no aspect of Rourke's work was more irritating than this tendency. It revealed her need "to discover a rich American heritage" though she had to fabricate it by herself. And so, in Rubin's view, Rourke's unrestricted tradition-inventing (examples are provided) represents "a variation on [her] adoption of the role of myth-maker" so that she might "strengthen the basis for art and social unity."

Rubin's speculations on Rourke's self-scrutiny, in connection with her achievements, are more candid and accordingly more painful than the commentary of any other serious critic of Rourke that I have read. What was the reason, Rubin wondered, for the divergence between the author's "conception of herself as a scholar and her choice of popular writing style" (including a carelessness in handling bibliographical citation)? Her concealing the scholarly research that went into her books, Rubin found, seems even harder to explain, given Rourke's "own awareness that other scholars did not take her work seriously." Her applications for Guggenheim and Carnegie fellowships were turned down time after time, and "academic historians" paid little if any attention to her work. Rejecting the argument that Rourke chose to write for a popular (including juvenile) market because she needed the money, Rubin suggested instead that Rourke's concept of tradition was at least a partial answer to the question of why she wrote in such a manner. Writing *about* the people and their common tradition(s) meant to Rourke: being part of them and writing *for* them in their own terms, with no intellectual barriers.

As regards the sociopolitical implications of Rourke's endeavors (recall that Rourke's important work, *Trumpets* excepted, was produced in the decade of the 1930s), Rubin made a number of points about utility value. Far too little attention has been given to the essential usefulness to all strata of the American public, of Rourke's program—and the following excerpted comments are particularly apt. At the time Rourke wrote, "the socialist left" offered "proposals for collective action"; Rourke did not by any means propose political action through collective effort. To her, tradition could be a basis for saving, or preserving, society—but her interpretation of how this might come about "was highly unprogrammatic, individualistic, and vague." There is a pronounced lack, in her writings, "of any awareness of antagonisms between rich and poor, labor and capital." Her emphasis on developing a feeling of a "common culture" virtually ruled out "class consciousness as a prerequisite for social change." But as far as Rourke's weakening her intellectual position by slanting her writings to a popular audience, by playing down her scholarly research, there was a significant benefit; she as well as others like her to some extent (Bernard DeVoto for example) would supposedly be in "the center of American life" and therefore safeguarded "from the intellectual's risk of isolation." In sum, however, as Rubin assessed Rourke's balancing—at the end of the 1930s— "moral, artistic, and political considerations," she argued that what Rourke achieved was "in her striving, not in the actual attainment of cultural unity"; this latter continued only as "a willed construct."[11]

It is time now to say something about Constance Rourke's importance as a writer, and what she has contributed to American literature and to literature generally. Her greatest achievement as a writer, in my opinion, is her calling into being the spirit of our people, the American character: her suggesting its broad, yet deeply rooted outlines, even in the face of certain very doubtful judgments. By calling her a comic poet, at the beginning of this chapter, I meant to hint at what would be said after the survey of critical and biographical commentaries. In the manner of an evocative, fanciful poet—a vatic interpreter or soothsayer (of sorts)—she discerned a deep truth about our diversified culture. Making a world, or making what may seem to be multiple worlds—with sets of prototypical figures: comic stereotypes, folk-hero giants, popular-success leaders like those in *Trumpets*—out of the wilderness of our earlier cultural history, is not a mere matter of simple imaginative creation. The poetic maker, the *poietes*, must do a special job: continually create this world-scene, sustain it with unceasing labor, lest it become lost. Thus I attach special meaning, at the risk of overinterpreting, to Rourke's reiterated concern in her various writings: there is still a great deal of work to be accomplished; "so much remains to be done."

As to Constance Rourke's contributions to our literature: her *American Humor*, I feel, for all its arguable judgments, remains her best piece of writing. Here, to a greater extent than in any other work, she provided students of American culture not only with an important new way of looking at the subject, but with a special vocabulary of applied terms for framing that view. This book, still available in paperback-reprint form, is—with all its paradoxical restraint in style, imaginative sweep in design, and eccentricity in execution—the product of a comic-poetic mind; and as such it remains ever fresh, in a manner of speaking, and bafflingly ambiguous.

Trumpets of Jubilee, though in style at least it often reflects more of Calvinism's severity and ponderousness than of the lightness of spirit suggested by the title, is also a marvelously evocative book. While it is clear that her five biographical subjects—three Beechers, Greeley, and Barnum—emerge *from* the people and, as huge popular successes, are very much *of* the people, they must also be considered as outstanding representative persons in their own right. Here, as she would do with folk-hero giants, Rourke conveyed the thrill she experienced when dealing with pop-up figures who thrust themselves sharply out of the printed page of legend and record, under the very eye of the reader. These five, in their own little world of new-era jubilation, show us the capacity for growth that is part of the American character: growth from frontier-community rawness to urban sophistication, growth out of Calvinistic mind-hobbling into a trumpeting freedom to entertain hopes of a better day.

What I take to be Rourke's second-best piece of writing is to be found in this book: her marvelous chapter on the life and hard times of Harriet Beecher Stowe, slave-woman (in effect) to masculine Calvinism, particularly as exemplified by her husband Calvin. In this saga of the bondage and qualified liberation of the famous daughter and sister of that rout of Calvinist ministers of the Beecher clan, Rourke showed how that lady came to be transmuted into Uncle Tom. And, an added source of pleasure, Rourke gave us insights into the affinity she herself felt with Harriet Stowe.

A third piece of writing that I feel deserves high praise is Rourke's *Charles Sheeler,* based to an extent on his own statements. But I do not wish to accept unquestioningly the revelation that Stanley Edgar Hyman received from this book: "a tradition lies not in content but in form." Not nearly enough evidence, in my view, has been advanced to show that a tradition lies only or mainly in form—and not (for example) in form *and* content. Sheeler's fine work with his "source forms" has not changed my mind, particularly in light of his emphasis on "the working of the parts toward the consummation of the whole." Parenthetically: the other revelation Hyman received, this time from *The Roots of American Culture*—and I feel the matter is relevant here—is that our "folk tradition is primarily abstract and not naturalistic." I see practically no real evidence for this at all. Hyman's random jumble of examples of abstraction: "a Jonathan Edwards sermon, a Navajo blanket, a John Henry feat, and a Vermont hooked rug,"[12] appear markedly unconvincing. Aside from its interesting and informative bits of art history from the late 1800s to well into the twentieth century, *Charles Sheeler* shows how *one* gifted artist-photographer worked with and within existing forms to create his own aesthetic renderings of line-and-space configurations.

This recap of Rourke's most important contributions (in my opinion) to our literature, in effect to the unearthing of our cultural roots, serves as finale to the story of her lifetime of purposeful, faith-keeping research and recording. Her determined spirit lives on, in her still available books (*American Humor, Trumpets of Jubilee,* and *The Roots of American Culture*) at the very least. And since "more remains to be done" than she could ever have dreamed, more even than her projected three-volume history could ever have included, I believe that someday important additions will be made to her pioneering studies.

Some encores are much more expressive if they do not follow shortly after the official stage program.

Notes and References

Chapter One

1. Robert E. Spiller, ed., *The Van Wyck Brooks/Lewis Mumford Letters: The Record of a Literary Friendship, 1921-1963* (New York: E. P. Dutton, 1970), pp. 43–44.

2. Constance Rourke archives, c/o Mrs. William J. (Linda) Butler, Tucson, Arizona.

3. F[rank] L[ee] D[u] M[ond], "Grand Rapids," in *Encyclopaedia Britannica* (1960), 10: 630; *AAA Tour Book: Michigan/Wisconsin*, (Falls Church, Va.: American Automobile Association, 1977), p. 28.

4. L[ee] A W[hite], "Michigan," in *Encyclopaedia Britannica* (1960), 15: 421; *AAA Tour Book:* Michigan/ Wisconsin, 1977 ed., p. 28.

5. Bill Granger, "Ford, Gerald," in *1974 Britannica Book of the Year*, p. 136.

6. From a 1974 Grand Rapids newspaper clipping sent me by a respondent; name of paper, date, and page number were missing.

7. Doris Branson, "GR Makes Its Mark in the World of Books," *Grand Rapids Press*, August 9, 1964, p.21; Elaine Clapp, "Art Gallery Gift Honors the Late Constance Rourke," *Grand Rapids Herald*, February 24, 1956, unpaged.

8. Constance Rourke, "Art in Our Town," *Nation* 150 (March 30, 1940): 424.

9. Ibid.

10. Rourke, "Art in Our Town," pp. 424–25.

11. Constance Rourke, "The Significance of Sections," *New Republic* 76 (September 20, 1933): 149.

12. I am indebted to the authors of the two unpublished biographical papers (referred to here, passim) given to me by Mrs. Linda Butler: "The Constance Rourkes" (1951) by Nelle A. Curry, and "Constance Rourke" [n.d.] by Margaret Marshall.

13. Lawrence A. Cremin, *The Transformation of the School: Progressivism in American Education, 1876–1957* (New York: Alfred A. Knopf, 1961), p. viii.

14. Ibid., p, ix.

15. Curry, pp. 16–18.

16. Marshall, pp. 19–21; Curry, pp. 5, 6, 18.

17. Quoted in Henry N. McCracken, *The Hickory Limb* (New York: Charles Scribner's, 1950), p. 210.

18. Marshall, p. 21.

19. Ibid.

20. Curry, p. 19, suggests a little of this: "There was the telling strain of age," etc. In fact, Mrs. Rourke would have been about sixty-three in 1915.

21. Curry, p. 7.

22. Quoted in Fred B. Millett, *Contemporary American Authors* (New York, 1944), p. 556.

23. "Constance Rourke," *Wilson Bulletin for Librarians* 11 (March 1937): 458.

24. The article, titled "A Distinguished Writer," kindly sent to me (by a lady in Grand Rapids) with other old newspaper clippings, was unpaginated.

25. Marshall, "Constance Rourke," pp. 2–3.

26. "Constance Rourke," *Wilson Bulletin*, p. 458.

27. Curry, p. 9.

28. Letter to this writer, Tucson, Arizona, November 9, 1974.

29. Lynn, p. xvii, n. The passage, quoted from *Troupers of the Gold Coast* (New York, 1928), is found on p. 246.

30. *Troupers,* ibid.

31. Curry, pp. 11–12.

32. Ibid., pp. 4–5.

33. Marshall, pp. 22–23.

34. Curry, p. 27; Marshall, p. 23.

35. Quoted in Stanley J. Kunitz and Howard Haycraft, *Twentieth Century Authors: A Biographical Dictionary of Modern Literature* (New York, 1942), p. 1206.

36. The *Grand Rapids Press,* March 26, 1941, pp. 1[?], 9.

Chapter Two

1. "The Porch," *Dial* 71 (October 1921): 418–19.

2. "Portrait of a Young Woman," *Dial* 71 (November 1921): 534–36.

3. Curry, p. 8.

4. Constance Rourke, "Voltaire Combe," in *"The Roots of American Culture" and Other Essays,* ed. Van Wyck Brooks (New York, 1942), pp. 253–54, 257, 259–61.

5. Constance Rourke, "Enchantment," *New Republic* 26 (May 4, 1921): 300.

6. "Private Life for Children," *New Republic* 27 (August 10, 1921): 294–96.

7. Constance Rourke, "Traditions for Young People," *Nation* 145 (November 20, 1937): 562–64.

8. Frank Freidel, "On the Home Front," in *We Americans*, ed. Thomas B. Allen et al. (Washington, D.C.: National Geographic Society, 1975), p. 392.

9. Allen Churchill, *Remember When* (New York: Golden Press, 1967), p. 122.

10. Constance M. Rourke, "Vaudeville," *New Republic* 20 (August 27, 1919): 115–16.

11. J. P. Chaplin, *Dictionary of Psychology*, new rev. ed. (New York: Dell Laurel Books, 1975), pp. 92, 201.

12. Stanley Edgar Hyman, *The Armed Vision: A Study in the Methods of Modern Literary Criticism* (1948; reprint ed., New York, 1952), p. 138.

13. Rourke, "Paul Bunyon," p. 179.

14. See C. G. Jung, *Two Essays on Analytical Psychology*, trans. R. F. C. Hull (New York: Meridian Books, 1956), pp. 141–43.

15. Curry, "The Constance Rourkes," pp. 7, 13.

16. Jung, *Two Essays on Analytical Psychology*, pp. 240, 245, 247.

17. Ibid., p. 247.

18. Constance Rourke, "The Significance of Sections," *New Republic* 76 (September 20, 1933): 149.

19. Hyman, p. 202. See also Edmund Wilson, *The Triple Thinkers*, rev. and enl. ed. (New York: Oxford University Press, 1948), pp. 197–212; Rod W. Horton and Herbert W. Edwards, *Backgrounds of American Literary Thought*, 3d ed. (Englewood Cliffs, N.J.: Prentice-Hall, 1974), chap. 10, "Marxism," pp. 211–53.

20. Rourke, "The Significance of Sections," p. 149.

21. Ibid., pp. 150–51.

22. Constance Rourke, "Artists on Relief," *New Republic* 87 (July 15, 1936): 286.

23. Rourke, "Artists on Relief"; Jerre Mangione, *The Dream and the Deal: The Federal Writers' Project, 1935–1943* (Boston: Little, Brown, 1972), p. 53.

24. Rourke, "Artists on Relief," pp. 286–88.

Chapter Three

1. Constance Rourke, *Trumpets of Jubilee*, ed. Kenneth S. Lynn (1927; reprint ed., New York, 1963), p. 322.

2. Will Durant, *The Story of Civilization*, pt. 4, *The Reformation* (New York: Simon and Schuster, 1957), p. 489.

3. Rourke, *Trumpets of Jubilee*, p. vii.

4. For a discussion of Constance Rourke's concern with "newness" here, in relation to the contemporary culture-pattern of renovation in the arts, see Kenneth S. Lynn's introduction to *Trumpets of Jubilee*, p. xii.

5. *Trumpets of Jubilee*, p. 321.

6. Ibid., pp. 322–23.
7. Ibid., pp. 4–5, 7–11.
8. Ibid., pp. 15, 17, 19–20, 25, 29–30, 47–56, 60–61, 65–66.
9. Ibid., pp. 27, 69.
10. Ibid., pp. 67–81 passim, and p. 82.
11. Ibid., pp. 37, 88, 89, 107, 108.
12. Ibid., pp. 89, 114–15, 117–20.
13. Ibid., p. 116. Some theological clarification is provided in *Trumpets of Jubilee*, pp. 31–32.
14. Ibid., pp. 120, 122, 125.
15. Ibid., pp. 127, 129, 135–36, 138–43.
16. Ibid., pp. 149–69. Henry Beecher's actual dealings with Elizabeth Tilton are generally overlooked by Miss Rourke.
17. *Trumpets of Jubilee*, p. 174.
18. Mark Schorer, *Sinclair Lewis: An American Life* (New York: Dell Delta Books, 1961), p. 476. *Trumpets of Jubilee* makes no mention of Sinclair Lewis's *Elmer Gantry*.
19. *Trumpets of Jubilee*, pp. 181, 185, 266.
20. Ibid., pp. 278, 279, 281–86, 298–99, 314.
21. Ibid., p. 24.
22. Ibid., pp. 41, 157–58.
23. Ibid., p. 200.
24. Ibid., p. 151.
25. Ibid., p. 201.

Chapter Four

1. *Troupers of the Gold Coast or the rise of Lotta Crabtree*, pp. 75, 111, 166, 167, 193, 236–38, 241. The book contains a number of photographic reproductions.
2. Curry, "The Constance Rourkes," pp. 8–9.
3. *Troupers of the Gold Coast*, pp. 255–56, v.

Chapter Five

1. Marshall, "Constance Rourke," p. 1.
2. Curry, p. 1.
3. Letter to this writer, Grand Rapids, Michigan, March 14, 1973.
4. *American Humor: A Study of the National Character* (1931; reprint ed., New York, 1959), p. x.
5. Ibid., pp. 12–13, 155–56.
6. Ibid., pp. 82, 132, 156, 202, 220, 230, 280.
7. Ibid., pp. 10–12.
8. Ibid., pp. 16–17.
9. Ibid., pp. 35–37, 40–43, 53.
10. Ibid., pp. 80–83, 86, 88, 90–92.

11. Ibid., pp. 107, 112, 114-18 passim.

12. Ibid., pp. 131-33, 136.

13. Ibid., pp. 138, 152–55, 157–59, 162, 202.

14. Ibid., pp. 149, 157, 266, 279–80, 288.

15. Ibid., pp. 173, 175–76, 267, 271–72, 274–79.

16. Curry, pp. 23–24.

17. Rourke, *American Humor*, pp. 165–67, 176–78, 181–88, 190, 191, 195–97, 200–201, 211–12, 223, 238, 243, 245, 288, 290–91.

18. Ibid., pp. 169, 197, 277, 285.

19. Ibid., p. 302.

Chapter Six

1. Lewis Mumford, "The Cultural Bases of America," *Saturday Review of Literature* 25 (August 15, 1942): 3.

2. Constance Rourke, *Davy Crockett* (New York, 1934), pp. 75, 224.

3. Constance Rourke, *Audubon* (New York, 1936), p. 319.

4. Ibid., pp. 285–86, 290, 304, 316.

5. Ibid., p. 286.

6. Ibid., pp. 58, 191–92, 287, 293, 307-08.

7. Constance Rourke, *Charles Sheeler* (New York, 1938), pp. 5, 51, 57, 115–16, 130.

8. Ibid., pp. 96, 113, 69, 110, 120, 195, 97, 70–71, 79, 77, 113, 188.

9. Van Wyck Brooks, Preface to *"The Roots of American Culture" and Other Essays* by Constance Rourke (New York, 1942), pp. v–xii.

10. Ibid., pp. 294–95, 278–79, 22, 26, 16, 51, 294, 277, 28–29, 31, 40–41, 224–25, 292–93.

Chapter Seven

1. An excellent survey of the famous attack on poetry in Plato's *Republic* is given in David Daiches, *Approaches to Literature* (Englewood Cliffs, N.J.: Prentice-Hall, 1956), pp. 3–22, particularly the concluding paragraph on p. 22.

2. Lewis Mumford, p. 3.

3. Alfred Kazin, "The Irreducible Element," *New Republic* 107 (August 31, 1942): 259–60.

4. Margaret Marshall, "Constance Rourke in the Critics' Den," *Nation* 155 (October 24, 1942): 418–20.

5. Alfred Kazin, "Constance Rourke: Reply from the Critics' Den," *Nation* 155 (November 14, 1942): 523; Margaret Marshall, "Miss Marshall's Rebuttal," *Nation* 155 (November 14, 1942): 523.

6. "Rourke, Constance Mayfield," *The National Cyclopaedia of American Biography* (1945).

7. Hyman, *The Armed Vision*, pp. 127, 131, 141.

8. Kenneth S. Lynn, introduction to *Trumpets of Jubilee*, p. xv.

9. Kenneth S. Lynn, "Rourke, Constance Mayfield," in *Notable American Women 1607–1950*, vol. 3 (1971).

10. Marie Caskey, "Rourke, Constance Mayfield," *DAB*, supp. 3, *1941–1945* (1973).

11. Joan Shelley Rubin, "A World Out of a Wilderness: Constance Rourke and the Search for a Usable Past" (Ph.D. diss., Yale University, 1974), pp. 159, 161, 163, 177–79, 202–03, 209, 269. References are to Rubin's dissertation rather than to her somewhat modified version in her book, *Constance Rourke and American Culture* (Chapel Hill, N.C.: The University of North Carolina Press, 1980), since the latter appeared after the present study was completed.

12. Hyman, *The Armed Vision*, p. 133.

Selected Bibliography

A very extensive bibliography of Miss Rourke's "readily accessible periodical writing," in addition to her books, is given in Ms. Rubin's 1974 Yale dissertation, *A World Out of a Wilderness: Constance Rourke and the Search for a Usable Past*, on pp. 271–79, and in her *Constance Rourke and American Culture* (Chapel Hill, 1980), pp. 215–32. I am grateful that the spadework leading to an eventual complete Rourke bibliography has been so well handled, and wish to add a note of thanks to Ms. Rubin. As far as Miss Rourke's journalistic pieces are concerned, in connection with my primary sources, I shall concentrate only on the more important articles, generally omitting the dozens of book reviews and the items in long out-of-print periodicals such as the *Freeman*. Published articles later appearing in book form (i.e., *Trumpets of Jubilee, The Roots of American Culture*) will not be listed separately.

PRIMARY SOURCES

1. Books

Trumpets of Jubilee. 1927. Reprint with Introduction by Kenneth S. Lynn. New York: Harcourt, Brace & World, Harbinger Books, 1963. Essays on Henry Ward Beecher, Harriet Beecher Stowe, Lyman Beecher, Horace Greeley, P. T. Barnum.

Troupers of the Gold Coast or the rise of Lotta Crabtree. New York: Harcourt, Brace, 1928.

American Humor: A Study of the National Character. 1931. Reprint. New York: Harcourt Brace Jovanovich, Harvest Books, 1959.

Davy Crockett. New York: Harcourt, Brace, 1934.

Audubon. New York: Harcourt, Brace, 1936.

Charles Sheeler: Artist in the American Tradition. New York: Harcourt, Brace, 1938.

"The Roots of American Culture" and Other Essays. Edited with preface by Van Wyck Brooks. 1942. Reprint. New York: Harcourt, Brace & World, Harvest Books, 1942.

2. Short Pieces

"The Rationale of Punctuation." *Educational Review* 50 (October 1915): 246–58.

"Vaudeville." *New Republic* 20 (August 27, 1919): 115–16.

"Paul Bunyon." *New Republic* 23 (July 7, 1920): 176–79.

"Portrait of a Home Town." *New Republic* 25 (February 23, 1921): 369–71.

"Private Life for Children." *New Republic* 27 (August 10, 1921): 294–96.

"The Porch." *Dial* 71 (October 1921): 418–22.

"Portrait of a Young Woman." *Dial* 71 (November 1921): 534–36.

"The Genius of the Novel." *New Republic* 29 (January 4, 1922): 149–51.

"Our Comic Heritage." *Saturday Review of Literature* 7 (March 21, 1931): 678–79.

"The Significance of Sections." *New Republic* 76 (September 20, 1933): 148-51.

"The National Folk Festival." *New Republic* 79 (May 30, 1934): 72–73.

"The Noble Sport of Ballad Hunting." *Nation* 139 (August 15, 1934): 192-93.

"Stowe, Harriet Beecher." In *Encyclopaedia of the Social Sciences*, vol. 14 (1934). P. 414.

"Examining the Roots of American Humor." *American Scholar* 4 (Spring 1935): 249–52, 254.

"The National Folk Festival." *New Republic* 83 (June 5, 1935): 102–3.

"Artists on Relief." *New Republic* 87 (July 15, 1936): 286–88.

"Index of American Design." *Magazine of Art* 30 (April 1937): 207–11, 260.

"Traditions for Young People." *Nation* 145 (November 20, 1937): 562–64.

"In Time of Hesitation." *Nation* 148 (February 18, 1939): 206–7. A review of Lewis Mumford's political manifesto, *Men Must Act*.

"Art in Our Town." *Nation* 150 (March 30, 1940): 424–25.

I shall not list here, as individual items, the personal correspondence relating to Constance Rourke and her friends—generously made available to me by Mrs. Linda Butler and others; nor shall I list the clippings from the *Grand Rapids Press* and the *Grand Rapids Herald*, likewise given to me by the kind ladies of Grand Rapids.

SECONDARY SOURCES

CASKEY, MARIE. "Rourke, Constance Mayfield." *DAB, supp. 3, 1941–1945* (1973). Pp. 672–73. A short biographical note.

"Constance Rourke." *Wilson Bulletin for Librarians* 11 (March 1937): 458. A short biographical note.

CURRY, NELLE A. "The Constance Rourkes." Unpublished essay, creative writing class, University of Michigan, Summer 1951. An excellent source of personal background information on Constance Rourke and her mother, this essay won an Avery Hopwood Summer Award in Creative Writing.

HYMAN, STANLEY EDGAR. "Constance Rourke and Folk Criticism." In *The Armed Vision: A Study in the Methods of Modern Literary Criticism.* 1948; Reprint. New York: Alfred A. Knopf, 1952. Pp. 127–41. The standard introduction to Miss Rourke's work, this essay also embraces a wealth of scholarship in the areas of myth, ritual, anthropology, and the various schools of criticism that have a bearing on folk criticism.

KAZIN, ALFRED. "The Irreducible Element." *New Republic* 107 (August 31, 1942): 259–60. A review of Rourke's *The Roots of American Culture,* and an overall assessment of her work: not strongly supportive.

KUNITZ, STANLEY J. and HAYCRAFT, HOWARD. "Constance Rourke." In *Twentieth Century Authors: A Biographical Dictionary of Modern Literature.* New York: H. W. Wilson, 1942. Pp. 1206–7. A short biographical note, with some interesting comments by Miss Rourke, written shortly before her death.

"Letters to the Editors." *Nation* 155 (November 14, 1942): 523–24. An exchange of letters between Alfred Kazin and Margaret Marshall: Kazin protesting that he does have a high regard for Miss Rourke's work, despite his qualifications in a book review of *The Roots of American Culture,* and Miss Marshall angrily accusing him of undervaluing Rourke.

LYNN, KENNETH S. "Constance Mayfield Rourke." In *Notable American Women 1607–1950.* Vol. 3. Edited by Edward T. James et al. Cambridge: Harvard University Press, Belknap Press, 1971. Pp. 199–200. A biographical note with an apparent error: Miss Rourke's father, from the evidence made available to me, had *not* been a lawyer, as Lynn states. There are also some arguable judgments, favorable and unfavorable, on her books.

MARSHALL, MARGARET. "Constance Rourke: Artist and Citizen." *Nation* 152 (June 21, 1941): 726–28. A tribute to Miss Rourke, written not long after her death.

———. "Constance Rourke." Unpublished essay, [n.d.]. A very informative biographical sketch, written from the author's personal knowledge of Miss Rourke.

———. "Constance Rourke in the Critics' Den." *Nation* 155 (October 24, 1942): 418–20. Another posthumous appreciation of Rourke's work, and an attack on those critics, including Alfred Kazin, who did not respond positively enough.

MILLETT, FRED B. "Constance (Mayfield) Rourke." In *Contemporary American Authors.* New York: Harcourt, Brace and Company, 1944. Pp. 556–57. A short biographical note.

MUMFORD, LEWIS. "The Cultural Bases of America." *Saturday Review of Literature* 25 (August 15, 1942): 3–4. A posthumous tribute to Rourke and her achievement, with special reference to *The Roots of*

American Culture, and couched (to a certain extent) in political terms.

"Rourke, Constance Mayfield." *The National Cyclopaedia of American Biography* (1945). Vol. 32. P. 100. A short biographical note.

RUBIN, JOAN SHELLEY. "A World Out of a Wilderness: Constance Rourke and the Search for a Usable Past." Ph.D. dissertation, Yale University, 1974. An extensive critical survey of Rourke's treatment of the American artist's position in America, vis-à-vis comparable positions taken by other important critics, Mumford, Brooks, Matthiessen, sen, DeVoto, Parrington, et al. Rubin makes use of the unpublished Rourke papers in Carbondale, Illinois.

————. *Constance Rourke and American Culture.* Chapel Hill: University of North Carolina Press, 1980. An expanded version of Rubin's dissertation (see above). A chapter on Rourke's life has been added, and there are photographic illustrations of Rourke and her mother.

Index